To Mr. Irving Cassini, Administrator

You are, beyond question, the
ablest and most versatile administrator
I have known, combining in equal
measures the rare qualities of intellect
and feeling, verbal skill and command
of the written word, generosity and a
sense of justice, tact and freedom from
sham, tirelessness and thoughtfulness.

You know where the above tribute is
taken from, and to whom it was
originally addressed.

June 28, 1968

SUNDAY MATINEE, MAY 7, 1967 AT 3:00 P.M.

IN MEMORIAM: Beryl Rubinstein (1898-1952)

CELIA HUAN

Pianist

PROGRAM

Man of Honor, Man of Peace

The Life and Words of

Adlai Stevenson

MAN OF HONOR

The Life and Words of

By the Editors of COUNTRY BEAUTIFUL
Editorial Direction: Michael P. Dineen
Edited by Robert L. Polley
Art Direction and Design by Robert W. Pradt
Contributing Editor: Frank Sullivan

Published by
G. P. Putnam's Sons, New York
In association with
Country Beautiful Foundation, Inc.,
Waukesha, Wisconsin

MAN OF PEACE
ADLAI STEVENSON

Country Beautiful: Michael P. Dineen, *Publisher and Editorial Director;* Robert L. Polley, *Executive Editor;* Robert W. Pradt, *Art Director;* Charles R. Fowler, *Managing Editor;* Kenneth L. Schmitz, James H. Robb, *Senior Editors;* Bernard J. Connell, *Administration;* Robert Fehring, *Art Assistant;* Sharon G. Armao, Vicki Russi, *Assistants.*

COUNTRY BEAUTIFUL Magazine is published by Country Beautiful Foundation, Inc., 24198 W. Bluemound Rd., Waukesha, Wis., a nonprofit organization dedicated to strengthening and preserving the physical, cultural and moral values of America and other nations of the world.

PHOTO CREDITS

CONTENTS

Preface ...... *President Lyndon B. Johnson* 9

Introduction ...... *Stewart L. Udall, Secretary of the Interior* 10

I THE STEVENSON IDEALS 15

II THE HOPES OF ADLAI STEVENSON 39

III STEVENSON AND THE AMERICAN PEOPLE 63

IV THE STEVENSON STYLE 73

Epilogue 90

Memorial Statement ...... *U.N. Secretary General U Thant* 96

Afterword ...... *Vice President Hubert H. Humphrey* 98

PREFACE

The flame which illuminated the dreams and expectations of an entire world is now extinguished. Adlai Stevenson of Illinois is dead.

His great hero, Abraham Lincoln, said at the beginning of his political career that "I have no other ambition so great as that of being truly esteemed of my fellow men, by rendering myself worthy of their esteem."

And although his disappointments were many, in this, like Lincoln, he was vindicated.

Like Lincoln he was rooted in America's heartland, yet his voice reached across every boundary of nation and race and class.

Like Lincoln he was a great emancipator. It was his gift to help emancipate men from narrowness of mind and the shackles which selfishness and ignorance place upon the human adventure.

Like Lincoln he will be remembered more for what he stood for than for the offices he held, more for the ideals he embodied than the position in which he served, for history honors men more for what they were than who they were. And by this standard he holds a permanent place on that tiny roster of those who will be remembered as long as mankind is strong enough to honor greatness.

It seems such a short time ago that out of Illinois came that thoughtful eloquence summoning an entire nation back from its dangerous drift toward contentment and complacency. For an entire generation of Americans he imparted a nobility to public life and a grandeur to American purpose which has already reshaped the life of the nation and which will endure for many generations.

One by one he sounded the great themes of our times — peace and justice and the well-being of humanity. And many men will labor for many years toward the vision and high purpose which was the generous outpouring of this man's heart and skills.

He was an American. And he served his country well. But what he saw, and what he spoke, and what he worked for, is the shared desire of humanity. He believed in us, perhaps more than we deserved. And so we came to believe in ourselves, more than we had. And if we persevere, then on the foundation of that faith we can build the wondrous works of peace and of justice among the nations.

He will not see that day. But it will be his day still.

LYNDON B. JOHNSON
The White House

INTRODUCTION

WORDS OF GREATNESS

Adlai Stevenson's last speech was made on the "Ten O'Clock" program of the British Broadcasting Corporation, Wednesday, July 14, 1965. The program had been taped earlier, and, when his British listeners heard Ambassador Stevenson's last remarks, he had been dead, of heart failure, for several hours.

In his last speech, he spoke not of his pleasure at renewing his many friendships abroad, but of his desire to return home and get back to his work at the United Nations, and of his hope that the action of the United States in Vietnam might "establish the fact that changes in Asia are not to be precipitated by outside force."

Opposite Ambassador Stevenson's remarks, British viewers could see on television: a drama of the French Revolution, in honor of Bastille Day, a semi-documentary "Men Against the Matterhorn," or a program about "preference and prejudice towards books and writers" called "Take It or Leave It." On Election eve, Monday, November 3, 1952, after his first Presidential campaign, Mr. Stevenson said: "I have said what I meant and meant what I said." And the accident of television programming around his final formal utterance seems rich in the symbolism of the man, and his message, and his place in our times, and his position in history.

Adlai Ewing Stevenson II was born in Los Angeles, California, February 5, 1900, where his father worked for a time as a newspaperman. But he grew up in Bloomington, Illinois, where the Stevenson family had settled in 1852, and where his mother's family had taken residence some twenty years before that.

His mother's family had emigrated to Pennsylvania from Northumberland in 1704, and the first of his American Stevenson ancestors had come to the same colony from Presbyterian Ireland in 1748. Both families fought in the Revolutionary War, were pioneers on the Kentucky-Ohio frontier, and early settlers of the flat, rich, farm land of Illinois.

A maternal great-grandfather, Jesse Fell, was a friend of Lincoln and an important force in Lincoln's campaign for the Presidency. His Grandfather Stevenson, for whom he was named, had been a Congressman, Assistant Postmaster General, and Vice President during Grover Cleveland's second term, from 1893 to 1897. His father was Secretary of State in Illinois, and a son is now in the Illinois legislature.

Mr. Stevenson wrote, in the "Introduction" to his *Major Campaign Speeches,* that he had been moved to many long thoughts because of a public opinion poll he read in 1943 "which reported that some seven out of ten American parents disapproved their sons going into politics or public service, or something like that." This is sometimes spoken of as the beginning of Mr. Stevenson's political commitment, but it seems unlikely that anyone growing up in the political household he grew up in would have ever lacked political interest, and a glance at his life shows that, from very early youth, Adlai Ewing Stevenson, Governor, Nominee for President, Ambassador to the United Nations, had long and fervently been committed to the causes for which, one might say, with deliberate ambiguity, he gave his life.

In a sense he had been dedicated to a special philosophy of politics before he was born. His grandfather, in a speech at the Chicago Auditorium, October 19, 1898, had said:

> Had our ears remained deaf to the cry of the stricken and starving at our doors, we would not have been guiltless in the high court of conscience, and before the dread judgment seat of history. The plea "Am I my brother's keeper?"— whether interposed by individual or nation,—cannot be heard before the august tribunal of the Almighty.

This quotation from the first Adlai E. Stevenson might serve as well as any paragraph the second Adlai wrote to express the political philosophy of Governor-Candidate-Ambassador Stevenson.

In 1920 Stevenson and his sister were in Switzerland on holiday. His sister wrote their mother, "Ad told me a few nights ago that he wanted . . . to join the reorganizers of the Diplomatic Corps." He was only twenty years old, but the pattern of his major interest seems to have been established. Twenty-seven years later when President Truman appointed him an alternate delegate to the United Nations, Senator Arthur Vandenberg (though a Republican) wrote to the future Democratic candidate for the Presidency: "when I was asked for recommendations . . . I put your name down as a 'must.' I wish you were devoting all your time to our foreign affairs at a high level in the State Department."

When Mr. Stevenson finished law school and had been admitted to the Illinois bar in 1926, he got himself accredited as a foreign correspondent with International News Service and set out for Europe. The Soviet Union at that time was almost completely closed to foreigners and no interviews were coming out of the Kremlin, but Mr. Stevenson hoped that he might somehow manage to talk to the Soviet Foreign Minister, Georgi Chicherin.

He didn't get his interview, but—and it was something of a triumph—he did manage, with great patience and considerable luck, to enter Russia through the Black Sea port of Batum, to cross the Caucasus to the Caspian, to travel locked in a slow train to Moscow where he spent a month of studious sightseeing and frustrating outeroffice-sitting and then finally to return home by way of Leningrad, Finland and Sweden. In that year of 1926 he had said that he wanted to talk to the Soviet people to bring "a new approach to breaking the log jam."

He returned to the Soviet Union 32 years later; this time he had his talk, a long one, not with the Foreign Minister, but with Chairman Nikita Khrushchev, and with many other Soviet citizens distantly scattered over that wide country and widely separated by age, opportunity, outlook, and position.

On returning from Russia to the United States he wrote:

> It is important, I believe, for us to make every possible effort to lessen their ignorance of our country and its democratic way of life. But likewise we need to study them hard and try by every means for better understanding and deeper appreciation. . . .

> What individual freedom under law means, is hard for people who have never had it to understand, but it is our most precious possession, and we should be proud and eager to exhibit it; besides it is the best hope for the future.

Mr. Stevenson was still trying to break the log jam, which by now has dammed (or damned) the current of our life.

Mr. Stevenson acquired early, and never faltered in, a belief in the power of reasonable discussion. Thirty-two years before his conversation with Chairman Khrushchev, foreign correspondent Stevenson had filed an article from Europe to be printed in the family newspaper, the Bloomington *Daily Pantagraph,* in which he wrote:

> Historically, suppression leads to violence. Taking away free speech is taking away the safety valve. . . . Imagine being liable to imprisonment for the mere expression of an antipathetic point of view, no matter how sincere!

When Mr. Stevenson returned to Chicago in 1926 he began to practice law. He married Miss Ellen Borden in 1928. They had three sons: Adlai Ewing III, Borden and John Fell.

In 1933 Mr. Stevenson was called to Washington to work in the Agricultural Adjustment Administration. With repeal of the 18th Amendment, he became assistant general counsel for the Federal Alcohol Control Administration. In 1935 he returned to Chicago and his law practice.

Mr. Stevenson's background, income, and education brought him naturally into accepted participation in community affairs. His inclinations, however, expanded his interest in the Chicago Council on Foreign Relations. He became its president, and by the late 1930s he was its principal spokesman, and speaking for its principles of internationalism became, rather than the practice of law, his principal occupation.

Colonel Frank Knox, publisher of the *Chicago Daily News,* knew Mr. Stevenson and shared the younger man's conviction that "isolation" was morally wrong, and, however politically expedient in some parts of the Midwest, it was a dangerous policy for this country to pursue. Colonel Knox became Secretary of the Navy in 1940, and, after a year of Chicago-based involvement by Mr. Stevenson in the affairs of the Navy, he brought Mr. Stevenson to Washington in 1941, where he was a man of all work for the Navy, the Foreign Economic Administration, the War Department and the State Department. In 1945 he became senior advisor to the United States delegation to the United Nations.

A law school student at the age of 24, Adlai Stevenson relaxed in a wicker lawn chair in the back yard of the Stevenson home in Bloomington, Illinois.

In the spring of 1947 friends of Mr. Stevenson began a good-willed, but essentially amateurish, campaign to make him a United States Senator. By the next year their determination had put him into the race for Governor of Illinois, and their zeal and their candidate's understanding, honesty, good name and energy, elected him by the largest plurality in the history of the state.

He was a fine Governor: efficient, imaginative and uncorruptible. In 1952, by what seems inevitability rather than design—and without Mr. Stevenson's active cooperation—he became the Democratic nominee for President.

He was defeated. In 1956 he actively sought the Presidential nomination, again received it with the same result. In 1960 some of his friends tried to snatch a third nomination away from an unwilling convention and thrust it upon an uncooperative Stevenson. Reports have it that his 1948 campaign for Governor of Illinois was a model of confusion from which no cluttering inconsequence was missing, but the bid to nominate him in 1960 surpassed even this inspired disorder with a positive and phrenetic disorganization. Senator Eugene McCarthy of Minnesota, a few hours before he placed Stevenson's name in nomination before the 1960 convention in the Los Angeles Sports Arena, said: "Usually these things turn into a war party of chiefs without any Indians; but this Stevenson draft here is a strictly all Indian operation."

President Kennedy named Governor Stevenson to the post of Ambassador to the United Nations—the position he held when he died.

Adlai Stevenson will be remembered by many because of his prose style, about which the first thing to be said is that it sparkled, not so much because of his choice of the words he uttered, but because of the thought he expressed. A comment like: "We dare not just look back on great yesterdays. We must look forward to great tomorrows"—will survive intact the rough handling of transposition, paraphrase or translation into any language.

And the second thing about his style is that it was not an exotic foreign importation, but was part of the native idiom. He was prepared, he told Mr. Valerian Zorin, the U.N. representative of the Soviet Union, to wait for an answer "until hell freezes over."

Novelist John Steinbeck, in speaking of Mr. Stevenson's style which he admired: "A man cannot think muddled and write clear." Mr. Stevenson's writing was clear, and it was touched with magnificence; it grew out of his thoughts, and his thoughts were the best of American thoughts.

Called upon unexpectedly at the funeral of a neighbor to say something, he instinctively responded with the spontaneous poetry of the Illinois springtime:

It is April now and all life is being renewed on the bank of this river he loved so well. Here by the river with the spring sky so clear, and the west wind so warm and fresh, I think we will all be the better for this day and this meeting together. Everyone loved this man. He enriched others and was enriched. I think it will always be April in our memory of him. It will always be a bright, fresh day, full of infinite variety and the promise of new life. Perhaps nothing has gone at all.

And this — in his own words — seems as good a way as any to remember Adlai Ewing Stevenson, American.

STEWART L. UDALL
Secretary of the Interior

Peace and human dignity were ideals Stevenson and other world leaders sought in the U.N. An informal Security Council discussion involved (left to right) Abdul Monem Rafa'i of Jordan, Charles Yost of the U.S., Stevenson and Radhakrishna Ramani of Malaysia.

I
The Stevenson Ideals

To many people Adlai Stevenson became, in his own lifetime, a figure of greatness in the gallery of history. There was an agelessness about him coupled with finality and a strong hint of immortality. He was a man vitally concerned with the problems of his own day, but even this contemporaneity was recognized as being rooted in a timeless concern for timeless values.

People of many different ambitions and environments, even of different nationalities, identified with his values and took a patriotic pride in the reflected glory of sharing the principles about which he spoke and by which he directed his actions.

He was a hero in that he was a protector, a defender, an explorer of human dignity and a warrior against all the forces that would degrade it.

To many of his admirers his defeats seemed to be, rather than a denial of success, an affirmation of the persisting value of a principle that could and did survive undiminished and untarnished, despite the accident of popular rejection.

No one would seriously try to evaluate Adlai Stevenson in simple terms, but if we were to try to find one word with which to summarize his objectives, his principles and his personality, perhaps he could most accurately be called a "Humanist."

He was, by reason of his heritage and his education, in taste and temperament, in his actions and reactions, in his work and his recreation, in the things he appreciated, and in the things he avoided, everything that culture, taste, and conviction call "humane."

He was a man—a social, rational, risible animal. He understood that men are most productive when they stand together sharing skills and talents and ambitions. He understood that men are strongest by reason of their reasoning. And he could laugh, and only man can laugh, and only great men can laugh at themselves as he could.

It was this humanity of Mr. Stevenson's with which people identified, and out of it grew what might be called the two head-lights of his drive. Adlai Stevenson moved forward in all that he did following the illumination of twin principles: the dignity of man, and freedom under the law.

He felt that a man was worth, not only saving, but also, dignifying. He fought to protect him against disease and hunger and despair, but he also fought to give him a belief in himself and in his fellowman. He worked for foreign aid, for domestic programs of relief and rehabilitation, to feed the hungry and house the homeless and care for the sick and the elderly. He worked for the traditional freedoms to speak, to assemble and to worship, and for the not so traditional freedom to disagree and to protest. He believed in the sacredness of the human conscience and the right of a man to stand secure in his convictions; for, to Adlai Stevenson, a man acting as a man was the wonder of the world, and humanity was the most precious of possessions.

But to possess the fullness of a man's individuality required, he believed, a community of cooperation within the framework of the law. The rights of everyman were the only rights that protected anyman. Each man, by enlightened self-interest, pooled the resources of his skills in the reservoir of cooperative government, and Mr. Stevenson looked forward to the time when such government would not stop at the borders of separate countries.

He felt that any man who put himself above the law of his fellows, or any nation that put itself outside the common laws of truth and justice, or any system that sought to enslave mankind, had, each and all, by their actions been demeaned by their own attempts to degrade humanity.

Law must exist; it must exist for the good of those governed by it; it must grow out of an understanding of, and appreciation of, the dignity of the individual; these were the guiding principles of Adlai Stevenson. It was by these that he governed himself, governed the State of Illinois, led the Democratic Party, wrote and spoke to the citizens of the world, spoke and voted within the United Nations.

We have had our disagreements and we still continue to have them. What is important is not that we differ from time to time; but that we have gone on broadening the area of agreement, and in the process we have learned to understand each other. The way to collaborate is to collaborate. That is what this executive committee has done, and I believe we will continue to do so.

At the closing session of the Executive Committee of the Preparatory Commission of the United Nations Organization, London, England, Oct. 27, 1945

The record of the United States in internation organization speaks for itself. Its initiative and support of the United Nations and all its agencies is the best evidence of our dedication to the principle of internation cooperation.

UN, New York, New York, Nov. 11, 1946

... Do you doubt the power of any political leader, if he has the will to do so, to set his own house in order without his neighbors' burning it down?

... Better we lose the election than mislead the people; better we lose than misgovern the people. ...

I ask of you all you have; I will give to you all I have. ...

And finally, in the staggering task you have assigned me, I shall always try "to do justly and to love mercy and to walk humbly with my God."

Formal Acceptance Speech, Chicago, Illinois, July 26, 1952

And before I leave I want to say to you, shamelessly and sentimentally, that my heart will always be here in Illinois.

Illinois State Fair, Springfield, Illinois, Aug. 14, 1952

Stevenson's grandfather, Vice President in the Grover Cleveland administration, held him for a 1900 picture (top). Adlai at three (above).

In Illinois the independents—and I include in that term all those who wear a party label over their hearts but not over their eyes—now those people in Illinois shared with me, I think, certain ideals and objectives for government at all levels. We believed in these things:

Government—any government—is not an end in itself. It exists to serve certain human purposes. These purposes should be enlarged only with caution. Indeed, the effort should be always to leave as wide a range of activity as possible in private hands and to keep public intervention as far down the scale and as close to the people governed as possible.

What ought to be done by government for the public welfare should be done. There should be no wistful dragging of the feet or turning backwards to a dead, irrelevant past.

Government should be competent. Its personnel must not be under the heavy hand of purely political selection of influence. It must not be afraid of raising and spending money for worthy purposes, but it must detest and fear waste and dishonesty as ever present threats to the whole moral basis of government by the consent of the governed because people don't consent voluntarily to be cheated or abused.

We believe above all else that those who hold in their hands the power of government must themselves be independent—and this kind of independence means the wisdom, the experience, the courage to identify the special interests and the pressures that are always at work, to see the public interest steadily, to resist its subordination no matter what the political hazards.

Denver, Colorado, Sept. 5, 1952

There are powerful interests who interpret the election as heralding an open season for the retail and wholesale transfer to the states of our great national assets—the forests, the grazing lands, the water and the minerals. . . . I hope we don't forget that the public domain belongs to Democrats and Republicans alike, and, as Theodore Roosevelt warned us long ago, the descendants of both will pay the price if we do not preserve our heritage.

Democratic Dinner, Los Angeles, California, Feb. 26, 1953

. . . It is our obligation to ourselves and to civilization to see to it that every willing hand is kept at work.

Charlotte, North Carolina, April 2, 1954

It is only in the strength of freedom, in the fortitude and sacrifice of free peoples; it is only in the humility of all men under God that we can create a future not scratched from the wreck and the rubble of war or from the chaos of domestic disorder but rising from the love and faith and the devotion of unconquerable humanity.

Southern Democratic Conference, Miami Beach, Florida, March 6, 1954

My fellow-citizens have made their choice and have selected General Eisenhower and the Republican party as the instruments of their will for the next four years.

The people have rendered their verdict, and I gladly accept it.

General Eisenhower has been a great leader in war. He has been a vigorous and valiant opponent in the campaign. These qualities will now be dedicated to leading us all through the next four years.

It is traditionally American to fight hard before an election. It is equally traditional to close ranks as soon as the people have spoken.

From the depths of my heart I thank all of my party and all of those independents and Republicans who supported Senator Sparkman and me.

That which unites us as American citizens is far greater than that which divides us as political parties.

I urge you all to give to General Eisenhower the support he will need to carry out the great tasks that lie before him.

I pledge him mine.

We vote as many, but we pray as one. With a united people, with faith in democracy, with common concern for others less fortunate around the globe, we shall move forward with God's guidance toward the time when his children shall grow in freedom and dignity in a world at peace. . . .

Someone asked me, as I came in, down on the street, how I felt and I was reminded of a story that a fellow-townsman of ours used to tell Abraham Lincoln. They asked him how he felt once after an unsuccessful election. He said he felt like a little boy who had stubbed his toe in the dark. He said that he was too old to cry but it hurt too much to laugh.

Statement conceding election, Chicago, Illinois, Nov. 5, 1952 ,

It is always true that when the citizens of a democracy become apathetic, a power vacuum is created, and corrupt men, incompetents — sometimes called "hacks" — or worse, rush in to fill it. But today our situation is more dangerous than that. In ordinary times the corrupt or incompetent office holder can be suffered for a while and then ejected.

But these are not ordinary times. The world's fate hangs upon how well or ill we in America conduct our affairs. And if a mad man is elected trustee of a sanitary district, or if any able man in Washington is left to shift for himself in the face of unjustified attack, then our Government is diminished by that much and more, because others will lose heart from his example. So you, as educated, privileged people have a broad responsibility to protect and improve what you have inherited and would die to preserve — the concept of government by consent of the governed as the only tolerable way of life.

Princeton University, March 22, 1954

We vote as many, we pray as one ...

I want to do everything I can to keep our country free and strong; a land to which all people in the world can look in the future, as in the past, with respect, confidence and, if I may say so, with love.

New York, New York, Aug. 20, 1953

. . . We have been winning step by step, which is the best tribute to the success of our post-war policies of assistance and resistance and to the power of free people working together with resolution, fortitude and faith. In consequence the danger of war has diminished. . . . But this is no time to relax or lower our guard.

New York, New York, Aug. 20, 1953

Root out, I say, the agents of this satanic world-wide conspiracy [Communism]; disclose the mistakes and failures of the past; assess the responsibility, let the chips fall where they may. But for the love of heaven let us do it with dignity, objectivity and justice, and with some better motive than partisan strife that can only seriously weaken the U. S. in its struggle with the total evil that besieges the world.

No one wins this way. Suspicion of past Democratic mistakes is balanced by suspicions of present Republican motives. The people are confused, confidence in both parties undermined, the nation injured. The issue isn't which party detests Communism most, but how to deal with the serious problem of espionage in our Government. And it won't be resolved to the nation's advantage by shouting matches and degrading circuses for political profit.

Georgia Legislature, Nov. 24, 1953

But it isn't in the nature of party structure that covers a nation to have total discipline and total conformity of view. There are bound to be disagreements, and it is well there are, because self-criticism, conflict and controversy are not only the ingredients of democracy, they are also the ingredients of progress.

But we can and we do agree on a great many more things than we disagree on, and we need one another in order to advance the great body of ideas we agree upon. There is, I believe, a growing desire in both North and South to go forward together, without bitterness, in goodwill, mutual respect and with a decent concern for the opinions of one another.

Georgia Legislature, Nov. 24, 1953

Overleaf: Ambassador Stevenson voted in the U.N. Security Council on self-determination for Portuguese territories.

Means are as important as ends. Fear is poison. And American influence cannot rest on military might alone, for principles are power — the very power that distinguishes democratic freedom from Communist tyranny.

Democratic Dinner, Philadelphia, Pennsylvania, Dec. 12, 1953

Using weapons short of war, and relying upon our reluctance to embark on global war, the Communist imperialism will attempt to absorb country after country, to close the ring around us, and to decide the issue between tyranny and freedom long before a final outburst of atomic fury.

Southern Democratic Conference, Miami Beach,
Florida, March 6, 1954

America wants an affirmative program — some idealism, if you will — and the inspiration to seek continuous growth even if we sometimes falter in the effort.

Tell the free and self-reliant American people what tonnage of steel is needed for the sinews of a full-employment peacetime economy, what dams are required to irrigate the new fields that are needed and to turn the wheels in new factories. Tell them what housing we need to cure the loathsome disease of slums.

Ask them to invest in schools for our children and hospitals for our sick, at least some part of what they are investing in guns. They have more faith than some of their leaders. They will not accept a doctrine of frustration. They will respond. . . .

Charlotte, North Carolina, April 2, 1954

During a Michigan vacation, young Adlai Stevenson was photographed with his father Lewis G. and his sister Elizabeth.

22

Rambling lawns and massive shade trees surrounded Mr. Stevenson's early home in Bloomington, Illinois.

In years gone by we required only of our career servants, upon whom the successful operation of the huge mechanism of government depends, that they serve at considerable financial sacrifice and that they serve with little glory or public esteem. Increasingly, it appears, we also require them to run the risk of being branded as "subversive," "undesirable," as "security risks."

Princeton University, March 22, 1954

There is only one basic answer to America's short-term and long-term economic problems—to unemployment, to butter surpluses, the slums and all the others. That answer is that we have to use the richness of this country and our own richness as a people—and that we have to use them to the full.

Charlotte, North Carolina, April 2, 1954

We look to ourselves and we are not ashamed. We are proud of what freedom has wrought—the freedom to experiment, to inquire, to change, to invent. And we shall have to look exactly in the same directions to solve our problems now—to individual Americans, to their institutions, to their churches, to their governments, to their multifarious associations—and to all the free participants in the free life of a free people.

Columbia University, June 5, 1954

What's the matter with us anyhow? The usual diagnosis is ignorance and fear. Ignorance leads many to confuse ends with means, to act as though material progress were an end in itself rather than a means to great and noble ends. . . .

And ignorance begets fear—the most subversive force of all. If America ever loses confidence in herself, she will retain the confidence of no one, and she will lose her chance to be free, because the fearful are never free.

But I wonder if all of these alarming concerns are not America's surface symptoms of something even deeper; of a moral and human crisis in the Western world. . . .

. . . In our time, in spite of our devotion to the ideas of religious and secular humanism, I wonder if we are in danger of falling into a spirit of materialism in which the aim of life is a never-ending increase of material comfort, and the result a moral and religious vacuum.

Is this leading, as lack of faith always must, to a deeper sense of insecurity and a deterioration of reason? . . .

Since man cannot live by bread alone, is not the underlying crisis whether he is going to be inspired and motivated again by the ideas of the humanistic tradition of Western culture, or whether he falls for the new pagan religions, the worship of the state and a leader, as millions of believers in the Fascist and Soviet systems have already done?

Columbia University, June 5, 1954

Why did America adopt the concept of man's responsibility for his fellow man? Our decision that the well-being of the least of us is the responsibility of all of us was, of course, not merely an economic and a political decision; it was, at bottom, a moral decision. . . .

It rested upon the conviction that it's the duty of the Government to keep open to all the people the avenues of opportunity that stretched so broad and so far before us in the days of our frontier. It rested upon the conviction that the Government must safeguard the people against catastrophe not of their making. . . .

Instead of isolation, our [foreign] policy is total involvement; instead of non-cooperation we have been the prime mover in the United Nations; instead of neutrality we have organized the greatest defensive coalition in history.

. . . In the process America has fathered three unprecedented ideas; Lend-lease for Hitler's intended victims in war, the Marshall Plan for Stalin's intended victims in peace, and Point 4 to help underdeveloped areas. And to pay for it all Americans have borne a tax load. . . .

. . . Why have we done all of this? Some will say self-interest, and there is truth in that because Communism follows the geography of human misery. Some will say magnanimity, and there is truth in that, too. For it would have been easy to go home as we did after the first war, or go it alone as some of our people proposed.

Call it what you will; the point is to help others help themselves, to help make independence and democracy work, to share the burdens of the less fortunate, to raise the tide a little all around the world, lifting all of the boats with it, just as we have done at home. . . . As Edmund Burke said: "Magnanimity is not seldom the truest wisdom." . . .

Columbia University, June 5, 1954

But what we need in the future or we have in the past is government animated by a consistent and overriding concern for all our people, and not, . . . just for business and industry. For not only does such favoritism stir up corrosive division within the community, it is also in the long run self-defeating.

Democratic Rally, Minneapolis, Minnesota, Sept. 25, 1954

Without our intellectuals we would not have made the advances in science, medicine, agriculture and industry which we have made — advances on which we are dependent for our welfare and for our security; advances which have made us the envy of the world. To demean our intellectuals is to deny the very basis of our national greatness.

Democratic Rally, Detroit, Michigan, Oct. 2, 1954

The years ahead will test
to the utmost our resolution,
our will, our faith . . .

And certainly a politician would be wise to spend more time in reflection in this tranquil countryside and less time displaying his small wisdom about large matters.

An election tends, of course, to emphasize our political divisions. This is as it must be for to vote is to divide and in selecting one candidate or party we necessarily reject the other. An election is both a selection and rejection; it is a choosing up of sides.

But it matters greatly whether reason or passion guides our choice. Reason will enlighten and elevate our understanding and it will discover in controversy the springs of a new unity. Passion will poison the political atmosphere in which the nation must meet the tests of the future.

The fact is that we are Americans, first, last, and always, and may the day never come when the things that divide us seem more important than the things that unite us.

. . . It would be too much to hope that there might be an end to the extravagant and dogmatic claims that one party represents all that is good and the other all that is evil.

. . . The preservation and strengthening of America requires above all the preservation and strengthening of our mutual trust and confidence.

Democratic Dinner, Indianapolis, Indiana, Sept. 18, 1954

Our nation faces grim years ahead — years which will test to the utmost our resolution, our will and our faith.

Cooper Union, New York, New York, Oct. 30, 1954

Left: Stevenson's sister, Elizabeth Ives, co-authored a 1956 book, My Brother Adlai. Below: The oath of office was given to the United States U.N. delegation in a ceremony witnessed by President Kennedy.

During a 1953 world trip, Stevenson visited
the Shwe Dagon Pagoda in Rangoon, Burma.

Ambassador Stevenson called the Berlin Wall,
". . . one of the most depressing sights of my life."

. . . For the success of our democracy depends upon the extent to which politics can serve the end of education, of justice and of truth. . . .

Cooper Union, New York, New York, Oct. 30, 1954

When we vote, we affirm our faith as free men and women in free government and society. And the survival of free government is what the contest of the mid-century and the clamor about Communism is all about.

Cooper Union, New York, New York, Oct. 30, 1954

. . . While Communist ultimate purposes remain fixed, Communist tactics have changed repeatedly. It is my belief that we are seeing today a broad and important shift in Soviet tactics. . . . They have begun to switch to the social and economic battlefield and to try, through diplomatic means, to split the Western coalition. . . .

New Orleans, Louisiana, Dec. 4, 1954

26

We must all work together, lest we all perish together...

The challenge is not just to win elections. The greater challenge is to live in pride and in freedom in a future so precarious and so threatening that we can risk no missteps and no miscalculations. We need to unite our country, not to divide it; to heal our wounds, not to enlarge them: The times demand, not mistrust and suspicion and fear, but more mutual respect and confidence and understanding than ever before.

This does not mean a suspension of hard and healthy debate, for hard and healthy debate is the essence of democracy. But hard and healthy debate has to do with real problems. It has to do with legitimate differences in policy and program.... No one needs to invent issues or to misrepresent them or to falsify them. No one needs to make confusion a policy and corruption a faith.

... To say that one or another American lacks patriotism or favors Communism or wants to subvert our freedom — when his only crime is disagreement — is to shake our system to the foundations. If we lose our faith in each other, we have lost everything; and no party victory is worth this.

... Men may differ about issues without differing about their faith in America or their belief in freedom; that politics must be a means, not of compounding our weakness, but of consolidating our strength.

Cooper Union, New York, New York, Oct. 30, 1954

Nowhere is this responsibility more greatly needed than in the discussion of foreign policy. And nowhere is unity manifested in intelligence and harmony of purpose more important. I should add that unity — bipartisanship — can never be an end in itself. No man or party would be justified in surrendering principles he deemed essential to national honor and safety simply for the sake of harmony. But where the independence and survival of the nation may hang in balance, we must all work together, lest we all perish together.

New Orleans, Louisiana, Dec. 4, 1954

What, after all, does the country want in a government? It wants a government which can inspire unity at home, which will provide security abroad and which will maintain a growing, prosperous economy.

Los Angeles, California, Oct. 9, 1954

... Communism feeds on, but does not create, all the frictions and conflicts of our small world. ...

Kingston, Ontario, Canada, Oct. 15, 1955

At a New York City meeting, Stevenson, his son Adlai III and Francis Cardinal Spellman examined a page from the Guttenberg Bible.

27

*Mr. Stevenson and Eleanor Roosevelt
were long-time friends and shared the ideals
of service to humanity.*

The problems that we face are not easy; but they are not insoluble. Compared with the rest of the world, our lot is fortunate indeed. If we can be confident without being cocksure, practical without being cold-blooded, warm-hearted without being weak-kneed, and idealistic without being dreamy, we can promote within our own boundaries and help to promote throughout the world those conditions of peace and well-being toward which free men have aspired since the beginning of civilization.

. . . It is the time, as always, to remind ourselves of those higher standards by which alone mankind can measure up to its appointed destiny. Politics are mean indeed unless they be the vehicle to greater ends. . . . It will be only if we hold fast to what we believe, to our faith, regardless of provocations, that we shall know the full meaning of victory.

Brooklyn, New York, Oct. 26, 1954

. . . America was built by visionaries, and our visionaries have proved to be our most practical men. History does not record more visionary ventures than those that went into our making. Columbus was a visionary. So too were the Pilgrim Fathers and every immigrant that followed them to these shores.

The Revolutionary War, a ragged bunch of Colonials pitting their wills and nerves and little else against the world's greatest military power, was a visionary enterprise. Jefferson and Jackson, Lincoln and Teddy Roosevelt, and many more in public and private life [were also visionaries]. . . .

Democratic Rally, Detroit, Michigan, Oct. 2, 1954

I believe deeply that it is the first obligation of every citizen of this Republic to work for the full realization of the goals stated in our original charter — freedom and equality for all Americans.

Freedom as I understand it means that a man may advance to the limit of his natural endowment without hindrance because of his race or religion.

Equality, as I understand it, means that each citizen shall be judged on his own merits. And particularly it means that every citizen shall be guaranteed equal treatment under law.

Portland, Oregon, Feb. 12, 1956

Our God-given abundance is a strong weapon in our hands for spreading democracy and freedom at home and abroad. You who open the soil to the seed know the urge to abundance in nature's vast resources. Let us work together to spread its benefits, to build a higher and more meaningful standard of living for the generations which will follow us on this land.

Agricultural Field Day, Newton, Iowa, Sept. 22, 1956

Americans have never lived by bread alone, but by ideals and moral values . . .

. . . The more people who take part in the processes of American Government, the stronger it is going to be—and the better informed they are the better job of democratic self-government they are going to do. Democracy needs all of the political participation it can get out of just as many individuals and just as many responsible groups as is possible. . . .

Many of us, I think, have been disturbed in recent years by the implications of bigness—big business, big labor, big industry, big government, mass communications, mass mindedness—growing massiveness in everything. Little businesses, independent businesses are vanishing like the autumn leaves. And as labor and industry get larger the consumer gets smaller. He is fast becoming the forgotten man.

AFL-CIO Convention, New York, New York, Dec. 8, 1955

. . . The effective working of twentieth-century democratic capitalism in America depends upon full recognition that organized labor is an essential and a responsible partner in the economy and the community; that it is concerned not only with the problems of labor as labor, but even more with those of citizens as citizens, of people as people; and the hopes and aspirations of "working people" are the hopes and aspirations of all people.

AFL-CIO Convention, New York, New York, Dec. 8, 1955

The question is not whether we are for or against prosperity. The question is whether we are for or against doing anything about the fact that 30,000,000 Americans today don't have prosperity.

Yet the battle against insecurity is only half the battle for a better life. A full dinner pail is a necessity. But Americans have never lived by bread alone. We have lived by ideals and moral values.

AFL-CIO Convention, New York, New York, Dec. 8, 1955

We must look ahead now to the handling of new factors in America's exciting economic future—to automation, to the peaceful use of atomic energy, to other miracles of progress just opening up. They must be used to increase the standard of living for the many, not just the standard of luxury for the few. They must be used to produce more leisure and not more unemployment. And it will take some mighty careful planning, much more than there has been so far, to see to it that this progress of the future pays off in time—time for all of us—time to enjoy the really, really good things in life.

AFL-CIO Convention, New York, New York, Dec. 8, 1955

Ambassador Stevenson escorted Jacqueline Kennedy to the annual U.N. concert in December 1964.

29

There is a relation between legitimacy of power and responsibility. The insecurity of knowing that power must be gained by tricks and deception breeds dynamic words coupled with irresponsible action. But power which comes legitimately . . . can be responsibly exercised with reason, patience, prudence and wisdom. It is only from that sense of security that wisdom can be joined with innovation, that new paths can be explored with security.

New Orleans, Louisiana, Dec. 4, 1954

If we do not stand unequivocally at home for civil freedom, we cannot hope to stand as the champion of liberty before the world.

If we do not stand at home for equal rights for all our citizens, regardless of race or color, we cannot hope to stand as the champion of opportunity before the world.

If we do not stand at home for steady economic growth and widening social welfare, we cannot hope to stand as the champion of progress before the world.

We should stand for all these things because . . . they are our great sources of strength in world conflict. Unless we stand for them, our moral pretensions are hollow. Unless we stand for them, we have no hope of achieving the peace we long for.

New Orleans, Louisiana, Dec. 4, 1954

. . . We believe that the dream of a fearless, and a free and an equal society, first cherished within these shores, is more potent than ever and can be spread around the world.

University of Virginia, Nov. 11, 1955

It's a marvelous thing to be an American. And it isn't just a lucky break. It's an unresolved responsibility, a responsibility to make this country a sounding board for new ideas, a welcomer of everything free and hopeful, a generous nation, the eternal home of liberty, and the temple of Truth.

TV Address on a Federal Program for Education,
Milwaukee, Wisconsin, Sept. 28, 1956

Now thirteen years ago this winter I was in Italy. The war was on. It was a wet, cold, ugly winter. It seems a long time ago. Our men were fighting their way up a valley whose name you wouldn't remember unless you happened to be there. It was called the Liri Valley. It was a place of mud and blood.

I served through the war as a personal assistant to the Secretary of the Navy Frank Knox. And what I saw and experienced there in the Liri Valley was nothing very out of the ordinary as war goes and as I saw it in the Pacific and Africa and Europe. I mention it now only because I think it was there that I decided that after the war I would do what I could to help in mankind's eternal search for peace.

TV Address, Chicago, Illinois, Oct. 15, 1956

*Stevenson visited Dr.
Albert Schweitzer at his jungle
hospital in Africa.*

*Mr. Stevenson's grandchildren,
Adlai IV and Lucy, joined in the 1962
Illinois U.S. senatorial campaign.*

We dream of a fearless, free and equal world society . . .

The United States stands squarely for the rights of man, individual man, man himself, as against any tyranny, whether it be the tyranny of colonialism or the tyranny of dictatorship or the tyranny of the majority.

UN debate on the Congo, New York,
New York, Feb. 15, 1961

Let me make my meaning abundantly and completely clear, if I can. The United States Government believes, and profoundly believes, that the single best and only hope of the peoples of the world for peace and security lies in the United Nations. It lies in international cooperation, in the integrity of an international body rising above international rivalries into the clearer air of international morality and international justice.

The United Nations has not achieved perfection, nor has the United States, and they probably never will. The United States, like the United Nations, is composed of humans. It has made mistakes, it probably always will make mistakes; it has never pleased all people, it cannot please all people; in its desire and wholehearted determination to do justice it may offend one group of states in 1952, another in 1956 and perhaps still another in 1961.

But always the United States has tried, and we believe it will always try, to apply even-handedly the rules of justice and equity that should govern us all.

UN debate on the Congo, New York,
New York, Feb. 15, 1961

While I cannot fulfill your expectations of miracles to come, I can commit my country, my colleagues and myself, to a tireless effort to make the United Nations successful — to make this great experiment in international collaboration fulfill the dreams of its founders — that one day reason would rule and mankind would be liberated from the everlasting scourge of war.

. . . As to colonialism, my country fought colonialism in 1776, when, if I may say so, the ancestors of the authors of this statement in the newspapers and this resolution had scarcely stirred beneath their bondage. And we have fought it ever since.

My countrymen died to end colonialism in the Philippines, and my countrymen have assisted the Philippine people to attain their present high destiny of complete independence. And my countrymen have died to end colonialism in Cuba, though some Cubans seem to have forgotten it.

UN debate on the Congo, New York,
New York, Feb. 15, 1961

Below: Governor Stevenson cast his 1952 Presidential election ballot near his Libertyville, Illinois, home. Bottom: Stevenson and Senator Estes Kefauver, the 1956 Democratic Presidential nominees, received convention support from former President Harry S. Truman and Texas Senator Lyndon B. Johnson.

The United States desires to do everything possible to put an early and a sure end to the arms race, which threatens humanity, . . . We are eager to resume negotiations soon and under conditions which will produce results and not further disappointments. It is only through negotiations that we can make progress.

UN, New York, New York, March 30, 1961

The American people overwhelmingly agree that the United Nations is man's best hope for peace. But it is something more than that. It is our best hope for fashioning a peace marked with freedom and justice—a peace which accords with the aspirations of free men everywhere.

The United Nations—as an idea and as an institution—is an extension of Western ideas; of Western belief in the worth and dignity of the individual; of Western ideology. It is based on a Western parliamentary tradition. Its roots are in the Western ideal of representative government. . . .

The identity of the United Nations with our deepest convictions about the nature and destiny of man is a central fact we need to keep in mind as we move through a period of relentless turmoil and travail. . . .

As something of an expert in rebuffs and disappointments, I may be permitted to emphasize that our judgments about political institutions and processes must not be based upon passing gains or setbacks, but rather upon the basic concepts and the long range goals they are designed to serve. . . .

Anyone who doubts the potent if intangible force of the United Nations should consider the eagerness even of Communist regimes to join a club which is, and will continue to be, managed predominantly by its non-Communist members. . . .

The United Nations is like a spade; it is not self-operating. It is what we make of it, for purposes that we can find in common with our neighbors in the world. To adapt a wise remark by a wise Frenchman, the making of peace is not a matter of the nations' looking at each other but of their looking together in the same direction. . . .

. . . The United Nations at its best is not a formula for "stability" but a framework for change. All the world's tensions are not bad; some of the incentives of hope and the drives for self-expression and self-government are what makes the free world hum. It is a mistake, in my judgment, for us to see the United Nations as merely a desperate survival operation, without also exploiting its potential as a cooperative search for better answers to the overhanging question, "After survival, what then?" Peoples are best cemented together, after all, not by mutual fear but by mutual hope.

Before the Senate Foreign Relations Committee,
Washington, D.C., Jan. 18, 1961

We sympathize with the desire of the people of Cuba — including those in exile who do not stop being Cubans merely because they could no longer stand to live in today's Cuba — we sympathize with their desire to seek Cuban independence and freedom. We hope that the Cuban people will succeed in doing what Castro's revolution never really tried to do: that is, to bring democratic processes to Cuba. . . .

We have heard Dr. Roa's colorful challenges and his denunciation of the United States paper on Cuba as the [lowest] and most astigmatic literature he has ever seen. Well, when it comes to astigmatism, I would remind Dr. Roa what the gospel says in the Book of Matthew: "And why behold thou the mote that is in thy brother's eye but consider not the beam that is in thine own eye?"

Answer to Dr. Raul Roa, Cuban Foreign Minister,
the UN, New York, New York, April 17, 1961

But today's statesmen must seek to improve the state of the world as well as the state of the nation. If it were once true that decisions were based solely on the interests of the state, it is now equally true that power politics and war are anachronistic. Today the ideals of individual dignity and liberty, and a human community transcending national boundaries, are the growing notions and the unfolding hope of world community and peace.

In relations among men, it is not enough to help those who are at a disadvantage, but it is necessary also to save, and if possible to increase, their self-respect. . . .

. . . There is no group of people so mean and so humble that they have only to be pupils, and cannot in any respect offer us instruction. . . .

New York, New York, June 6, 1961

After listening to the Soviet speech, which we had already heard in the Security Council, I have concluded that there are two Congo problems: one in Africa and one in New York, and that the one in New York is, if anything, the most serious. . . .

. . . I wish the Soviet Union would contribute something to it besides obstruction and criticism. . . .

UN General Assembly, New York, New York, March 21, 1962

Above right: Stevenson was presented an appreciation award by Chicago Mayor Richard Daley on the observance of the 10th anniversary of the U.N. Right: President Lyndon B. Johnson and Mr. and Mrs. Adlai Stevenson III were present for the Adlai Stevenson memorial postage stamp announcement at a White House ceremony.

Our only permissible reaction to failure is a new dedication to success. We need to make better and fuller use of our procedures for peaceful settlement. And we should consider how those means can be improved. We should ponder over our recent experience and learn from it; for it would appear that institutions, like individuals, frequently have to learn, the hard way. . . .

What we need above all is a new and firm resolve to banish from this earth the technique of force and to substitute for it the techniques of peaceful progress. What in the end will be decisive is a change in the attitude of member states both towards injustices in the world and toward the use of force itself. . . .

But the lesson to be drawn is not that the police force should be abandoned in favor of vigilantism. The lesson to be drawn is that the law should be applied with new vigor, impartially to all alike, and in the interests both of justice and of peace.

The United States dedicates itself again to this purpose. We are confident that this is what the vast majority of the world's millions—both new and old—also want to do.

At the Recess of the 16th Session of the UN General Assembly,
New York, New York, Dec. 21, 1961

The Communists have catered assiduously to the impatience of students and intellectuals to see wrongs redressed and to their wish to employ their energies and imaginations in the interest of their fellow men. Communism sees in high-minded intellectuals and students in Latin America useful tools for launching the illiterate or semiliterate majorities in their countries on the road to Communist revolution. The vigor and effectiveness of the penetration into intellectual and student circles have clearly grown over the past year.

New York, New York, Aug. 5, 1961

Democracy takes into account the factor to which Communism seems to be invincibly obtuse: the unsearchable depths of the mind and spirit of man, who will forever thwart the attempts of dogma and ideology to predict him or to hem him in.

Anti-Defamation League of B'nai B'rith, New York, New York, Jan. 15, 1962

[In the U.S. the] last convulsions of a struggle over color are taking place. . . . The Russians must realize that they, if color is a determining factor, are in a small minority with us.

New York, New York, Oct. 14, 1963

I am far more concerned about the hundreds of Latin Americans flocking to Cuba for training in Communist theory and techniques and what they can do for the universal social revolution than I am about the Russian troops.

Speech to the Chicago Council on Foreign Relations,
Chicago, Illinois, Feb. 19, 1963

Mr. Stevenson and Dr. Jonas Salk, polio vaccine pioneer, received honorary degrees from New York University in 1955.

I am convinced that in the United Nations history for 1961—after accounting for all the faults and mistakes and all the criticism in which passion and partisanship have outrun knowledge—much will be found that was magnificent and perhaps decisive for the future peace of the world.

At the Recess of the 16th Session of the UN General Assembly,
New York, New York, Dec. 21, 1961

I do not assert that Communism must always remain a messianic faith. Like other fanaticisms of the past, it may in time lose its sense of infallibility and accept the diversity of human destiny. Already in some countries we see Communism subsiding into a local and limited ideology. There are those who have discerned the same evolution in the Soviet Union itself; and we may all earnestly hope that Chairman Khrushchev and his associates will renounce the dream of making the world over in the image of the Soviet Union. It must be the purpose of other nations to hasten that day.

But the day has not yet arrived. The conflict between absolutist and pluralistic conceptions of the destiny of mankind remains the basic source of discord within the United Nations. It has given rise to what is known as the Cold War. Were it not for this conflict, this organization would have made steady progress toward the world of choice and justice envisaged at San Francisco.

UN Security Council debate on the Cuban missile crisis,
New York, New York, Oct. 22, 1962

Governor Stevenson and poet
Carl Sandburg discussed their common
Illinois heritage during a
January 1949 meeting.

The essence
of democracy is
the dignity of man . . .

Today democracy here at home and around the world is being strained as never before.

Defining democracy is like squaring the circle—after centuries of labor, the mathematicians solved the problem by proving that it cannot be solved. And if you complain that that is a paradox, I will reply that democracy's greatest strength is in its acceptance of paradox—and in the room which it allows for the unimaginable, incommensurable possibilities of human nature. . . .

Communism has yet to be the popular choice of one single nation anywhere on the face of the globe. In the few places where it has extended its control, whether in Czechoslovakia, North Vietnam, or Cuba, it has been in the same classic role— as the scavenger of war and of ruined revolutions.

. . . The promised victory of Communism keeps on receding into the future. The juggernaut just does not jug. Either democracy is less bumbling than we fear, or Communism is less efficient than it claims.

Sept. 15, 1962

Rigid adherence to the law, to the Charter, is essential to the Charter's preservation. Once you begin to contaminate or erode or interpret the Charter too flexibly you very soon will have no sustaining body of legal structure to support the United Nations.

UN, New York, New York, Dec. 19, 1963

The ink was hardly dry on the Charter before Moscow began its war against the world of the United Nations. The very first meeting of the Security Council—and I was there—was called to hear a complaint by Iran that Soviet troops had failed to withdraw from the northern part of that country on the date on which they had agreed to leave.

UN Security Council debate on the Cuban missile crisis,
New York, New York, Oct. 23, 1962

. . . The essence of democracy is the dignity of man. We shall create a free world order on no other basis. If we attack Communism—as we must—for its contempt for political dignity, we must attack as unrelentingly lapses in social dignity.

It sometimes seems to me today as though running through all the great issues of the day—the anti-colonial revolution, the political contest with Communism, the unification of Europe, the clamor of poorer lands for advance—there [is] the underlying desire for some lasting realization of the dignity of man— man with a measure of political autonomy, man with the economic elbow room to live above the torturing doubts of food and work, man with the dignity to look his neighbor in the face and see a friend.

Convention of the Center for the Study of Democratic Institutions,
New York, New York, Jan. 22, 1963

And we would say to the enemies of freedom, whatever the magnificent ends they propose—the brotherhood of man, the kingdom of saints, "from each according to his ability, to each according to his needs"—[they] miss just this essential point: that man is greater than the social purposes to which he can be put. He must not be kicked about even with the most high-minded objectives. He is not a means or an instrument. He is an end in himself. . . .

Convention of the Center for the Study of Democratic Institutions,
New York, New York, Jan. 22, 1963

The threat to peace in Cuba comes not from the United States but from the Soviet Union. The threat arises from the extraordinary and unnecessary flood of Soviet arms and military personnel pouring into Cuba. . . .

If the Soviet Union genuinely desires to keep the peace in the Caribbean, let it stop this warlike posturing. This stuffing of Cuba with rockets, military aircraft, advanced electronic equipment and other armament is all out of proportion to any legitimate needs.

Answer to Soviet charges on Cuba, Sept. 21, 1962

. . . The maintenance of Communism in the Americas is not negotiable.

In reply to President of Cuba Osualdo Dorticos Torrado's
speech in the UN, New York, New York, Oct. 9, 1962

Five days after Ambassador Stevenson's death in July 1965, delegates to the United Nations met in the General Assembly hall for a memorial ceremony. A moment of silent tribute followed numerous eulogies.

II

The Hopes of Adlai Stevenson

A man often reveals himself more by the things he wants to do than by the things he does, or is, and Adlai Stevenson's hopes are easy to discover. Implicit in his early activity, and explicit in his later writing, is an overwhelming desire to present the world with a plan for peace, and an undiscouraged hope that the world would understand and pursue it.

It might be said in fairness that such a desire, such a hope, does not set any thoughtful man apart from other thinkers today. Today, one may presume, no one in a position to realize the consequences of nuclear war wants to provoke it. But Mr. Stevenson's significance is that his hopes were practical hopes, and his wishes not simply wishful thinking.

To him the desire for peace was neither a distant unattainable daydream, nor was it a self-actuating automatic guarantee against war. Peace, he felt, had to arrive soon or the world was lost, but it would not come by itself. It would have to be brought forward—painfully worked out through the reasoned plans of intelligent men, carefully protected by men of good will.

Because Adlai Stevenson was so obviously a man of intellect rather than appetite, so obviously devoted to the spiritual rather than the material, a very real part of his character was sometimes unnoticed. He was a hard-boiled realist who recognized that you can't get the attention of a hungry man by offering him food for thought.

To Mr. Stevenson it was obvious—as, strangely enough, it does not seem obvious to many others who view the world today—that it is better to be healthy than to be sick, better to be rich than to be poor. He was aware of, and shocked by, and frightened at the gap between the living standards of rich nations and poor nations. He observed that while the rich grew richer the poor grew poorer. And he concluded that this was the explosive mixture that could destroy civilization.

To preserve the peace a man must have a piece of something worth preserving. Mr. Stevenson recalled the history of other times and places when other well-fed societies were destroyed by hungry neighbors, and, by pointing out the dangers of national selfishness and international complacency, he tried to prevent history's repeating itself.

Mr. Stevenson had a great respect for American business and industry in its capacity to produce. He attempted to enlist business and industry in the cause of economic expansion. He urged the necessity of domestic growth based upon expanding power of individuals to become customer-consumers. He urged the further necessity of spreading this growth beyond the limits of this country and beyond the bounds of certain favored nations, and in this developing prosperity he planted his hopes for peace.

Mr. Stevenson felt that in this crusade for the necessity of peace through economic expansion, cooperation and contribution, his indispensable ally was an intelligent citizenry trained to look past immediate profit and beyond quick and easy answers. Reason tells us that we must have peace, and, since it will elude all else, the successful pursuit of it is possible only with the full cooperation of reasonable men.

To get such a rational society, Adlai Stevenson often directed his attention to education. Education was to Adlai Stevenson something which lifted a man to the great height of his full humanity. It gave meaning to life, and strength to democracy, and it offered the last chance for peace.

No one would suggest that the hopes of any man could be reduced to the desire for just one thing. But it is clear enough that Adlai Stevenson's desire for a just and lasting peace took precedence over most of the things he spoke of publicly.

It is also clear enough that his hopes for peace included many things: education that would produce reasonableness and reason that would beget action, expansion and a cooperative understanding of what it is to be a man, a cooperation that would allow men everywhere to realize to the fullest and highest the dignity of manhood.

Ambassador Stevenson addressed the U.N. Security Council on the Republic of Congo situation in early 1961.

UNITED STATES

It is a very solemn hour indeed, freighted with the hopes and the fears of millions of mankind who seek in us, the Democratic party, sober understanding of the breadth and depth of the revolutionary currents in the world. Here and abroad they see in us awareness that there is no turning back, and that, as Justice Holmes said, "We must sail sometimes with the wind, sometimes against it; but we must sail and not drift or lie at anchor." They see in us, the Democratic party that has steered this country through a storm of spears for twenty years, an understanding of a world in the torment of transition from an age that has died to an age struggling to be born. They see in us relentless determination to stand fast against the barbarian at the gate, to cultivate allies with a decent respect for the opinion of others, to patiently explore every misty path to peace and security which is the only certainty of lower taxes and a better life.

This is not the time for superficial solutions and for endless elocution, this is not the time for frantic boasts and foolish words. For words are not deeds and there are no cheap and painless solutions to war, to hunger, to ignorance, to fear and to the new imperialism of the Soviet Union. My friends, you know full well that intemperate criticism is not a policy for the nation; and denunciation is not a program for our salvation. Words that are calculated to catch everyone may catch no one. And I hope that we can profit from their mistakes not just for our partisan benefit but for the benefit of all of us, Republicans and Democrats alike.

Welcoming Address, National Democratic Convention,
Chicago, Illinois, July 22, 1952

I believe we are living in the twilight of the totalitarian gods; beyond the fury and the turmoil of our times lies an horizon of new hope for embattled humanity. With liberal faith, with cool heads, with warm hearts, we shall make that hope real for our nation and for our century.

Speech to the Liberal Party, New York, New York, Aug. 28, 1952

. . . The reflection of America is blurred and distorted. There is an impression that we are inflexible and erratic; that faith in cooperation is being replaced by belief in unilateral action — a readiness to go it alone. . . . There is an impression that "trade not aid" is becoming no aid and no trade.

New York, New York, Aug. 20, 1953

. . . It is well to try to see ourselves as others see us. Many think we are intemperate, inflexible and frightened. And people who have lived in insecurity for centuries don't understand how there can be insecurity and fear in America, which has never been bombed or lived in thralldom. Also, like ourselves, proud nations resent any real or suspected interference in their domestic affairs.

Radio-TV Address, Chicago, Illinois, Sept. 15, 1953

The door to the conference room is the door to peace...

What does concern me ... is not just winning the election, but how it is won, how well we can take advantage of this great quadrennial opportunity to debate issues sensibly and soberly. I hope and pray that we Democrats, win or lose, can campaign not as a crusade to exterminate the opposing party, as our opponents seem to prefer, but as a great opportunity to educate and elevate a people whose destiny is leadership, not alone of a rich, prosperous, contented country as in the past, but of a world in ferment.

And more important than winning the election is governing the nation. That is the test of a political party — the acid, final test. When the tumult and the shouting die, when the bands are gone and the lights are dimmed, there is the stark reality of responsibility in an hour of history haunted with those gaunt, grim specters of strife, dissension and materialism at home, and ruthless, inscrutable and hostile power abroad.

The ordeal of the twentieth century — the bloodiest, most turbulent age of the Christian era — is far from over. Sacrifice, patience, understanding and implacable purpose may be our lot for years to come.

Let's face it. Let's talk sense to the American people. . . .

Let's tell them then the victory to be won in the twentieth century, this portal to the golden age of man, mocks the pretensions of individual acumen and ingenuity. For it is a citadel guarded by thick walls of ignorance and mistrust which do not fall before the trumpets' blast or the politicians' imprecations....

Formal Acceptance Speech, Chicago, Illinois, July 26, 1952

If there is strength in unity there is weakness in disunity, and one thing is certain, the Communists will exploit every possibility of dividing America and her allies.

This as I see it is one of our greatest hazards in a world in ferment divided between the totalitarian peoples, the free peoples and the uncommitted peoples. Everyone does not share our views of Communism and its menace. . . . Nor do they think we are endowed with all the wisdom, power and morality in the world.

While there is much misunderstanding *in* America, there is as much or more misunderstanding *of* America.

New York, New York, Aug. 20, 1953

...We Americans are inspired by the challenge to bridge the gulf between what is and what may be. But much remains to be done in the South and elsewhere. . . .

Georgia Legislature, Nov. 24, 1953

There is no substitute for seeing with your own eyes and hearing with your own ears. I wanted to see and hear for myself. And what I have seen and heard [on a trip through Asia and the Middle East] is both encouraging and sobering.

New York, New York, Aug. 20, 1953

We owe it to ourselves and our anxious, weary friends to expose Communist intentions if we can . . . to reduce tension and restore hope where we can. The door to the conference room is the door to peace. Let it never be said that America was reluctant to enter.

Radio-TV Address, Chicago, Illinois, Sept. 15, 1953

What will it take to maintain economic stability? What is required of us? There are houses to be built and slums to be cleared. Our forests, public lands and parks need protection and improvement. We have watersheds to protect against the ravages of flood and erosion, and river valleys to develop. Roads, schools, hospitals are in arrears.

. . . Any future downswing in economic activity must be the signal for a prompt adjustment of tax burdens to release money for private spending. . . . Farmers, business men, home owners and consumers must be assured of adequate credit.

We must also consider how improvements in our Social Security system and farm program can better our defenses against depression. When a worker loses a job, he is not the only one who suffers.

The butcher, the baker, the grocer also lose a customer, and the chain reaction runs through the economy. It is the same when the farmers' prices fall.

There are few better forms of insurance against depression than a sound farm program. . . .

Democratic Dinner, Philadelphia, Pennsylvania, Dec. 12, 1953

. . . If our friends and allies can't find markets and sources of supply outside the Iron Curtain, trade with the Communist orbit will grow. I doubt if anyone is going to starve to prove to us how anti-Communist they are.

Democratic Dinner, Philadelphia, Pennsylvania, Dec. 12, 1953

As I see it our duty as citizens first . . . is not recrimination; it is not to defend or deny the past, for yesterday is irretrievable and the problems are now and tomorrow.

Democratic Dinner, Philadelphia, Pennsylvania, Dec. 12, 1953

It seems to me that the new weapons—even if we had a complete monopoly — are no answer to all the complicated aspects of this world-wide struggle, for armed aggression is only one of the many shapes of the Communist menace.

Southern Democratic Conference, Miami Beach, Florida, March 6, 1954

Mr. Stevenson discussed world problems with Israel's Prime Minister David Ben-Gurion (above) and Yugoslavia's President Tito (below).

... The central economic fact of our time is that this economy of ours cannot stand still; it must either grow or fall.

There will be two million more Americans a year from now, fifteen million more by the end of this decade. . . . We must have . . . more jobs immediately, and then more and more. . . .

Charlotte, North Carolina, April 2, 1954

The question is, I suppose, whether the human and rational emotions can be aroused instead of the animal and irrational to which the totalitarians appeal. But fill the moral vacuum, the rational vacuum, we must; reconvert a population soaked in the spirit of materialism to the spirit of humanism we must, or bit by bit we too will take on the visage of our enemy, the neo-heathens.

Columbia University, June 5, 1954

Government can't do all the things that need to be done, but it can, through the goals it sets and the policies it adopts, help all of us — business, labor, agriculture — to think and act in terms of growth and abundance. Conversely, Government can cut its commitment to the future and thereby the momentum of our forward movement.

. . . It seems to me a great issue hangs in the balance; whether democracy is going to be received as a means of hanging on to yesterday or as a way of meeting tomorrow.

America has everything it needs to keep on growing — to raise the standard of its living — to keep all of its hands at the job of production. It is inevitable that occasional mistakes will be made and that we will stumble. The key to America's future will not turn easily in the lock of today's troubled world.

Democratic Rally, Minneapolis, Minnesota, Sept. 25, 1954

Prosperity, like peace, is indefensible, and the most important thing to business and industry is and will remain a nation of customers with money in their pockets. Millions unemployed are more than a statistic; they are a mark of failure of our system that we cannot view with satisfaction because they aren't more numerous.

Democratic Rally, Minneapolis, Minnesota, Sept. 25, 1954

America wants and needs understanding and positive purpose, generously enlightened with idealism and the inspiration to seek continuous growth. . . .

Democratic Rally, Detroit, Michigan, Oct. 2, 1954

America has been called to greatness. The summons of the twentieth century is a summons to our vision, to our humanity, to our practicality. If these provide the common purpose of America and Asia . . . we need have no fear for the future. Because it will belong to free men.

San Francisco, California, Oct. 16, 1954

Soviet Premier Nikita Khrushchev and Stevenson talked informally after touring Iowa farms in 1959.

Whether we like it or not, the rest of the world makes comparisons between the U.S. and the Soviet Union. And while most of the non-Communist countries admire our free institutions, some people wonder whether freedom is a luxury beyond their means. If they feel free to choose between freedom and economic development, relief from want and misery, many will choose economic development. Too many of us think of the threat of world Communism only as a military threat. It is much more than that.

Because our success or failure depends on economic as much as military factors, our prosperity is as important to our security as our atomic stockpile, perhaps more so.

Democratic Rally, Detroit, Michigan, Oct. 2, 1954

... Strength is not an end in itself but a means to an end, we could explore with greater confidence the possibilities of negotiation with our friends, yes, and with our enemies — negotiations for settlements here and there and for safe and sound disarmament, thus inching our way along the weary path to peace. Negotiation without strength, which some of our European friends seem to want is madness. Strength without negotiation is futility. Negotiation on the basis of strength and solidarity is the only policy which can hold out to patient and suffering mankind.

San Francisco, California, Oct. 16, 1954

... Security and freedom in much of the world depends today more on economic progress than military defense. The number one problem in Asia today is not Communism but that millions of people want a better life and have discovered that poverty, hunger and pestilence are not the immutable destiny of man. If they can't make progress by the voluntary democratic methods of consent, they will turn to the involuntary methods of coercion, as China already has. ...

So our obligations are many and complex. Military strength, allied unity, economic growth — these I think are the solid foundations of the collective power of the free peoples.

New Orleans, Louisiana, Dec. 4, 1954

... As long as we maintain our own military strength at sufficiently high levels the chief threat in the next period will be Communist exploitation of social and political unrest. This analysis implies two main obligations for the United States.

... Our first obligation is to maintain our own strength and the unity of our coalition. ... Our second obligation is to show peoples struggling for economic and national deliverance that they can fulfill their aspirations better in association with free peoples and by the methods of consent than they can by submitting to the iron yoke of Communism.

New Orleans, Louisiana, Dec. 4, 1954

45

To match evil with good is our greatest challenge...

After the 1952 Presidential campaign, Mr. Stevenson conferred with Indian Prime Minister Jawaharlal Nehru.

I have always insisted that far more unites us, as a people, than divides us. And I have always regarded this, not just as a fortunate fact, but as a grim necessity for survival as an independent nation. If we cannot achieve essential unity, especially in the conduct of our foreign policy, then our divisions will expose us to ghastly possibilities of catastrophe in this troubled world.

New Orleans, Louisiana, Dec. 4, 1954

... To resist the provocation of retaliation in kind, to match evil with good, falsehood with honesty, is never easy and the results are not always reassuring. But this remains the greatest challenge to our political maturity. ...

New Orleans, Louisiana, Dec. 4, 1954

... Keeping friends these days calls for more statesmanship than challenging enemies, and the cause of world peace transcends any domestic political considerations.

Radio Address, Chicago, Illinois, April 11, 1955

... Teachers must be freed from the shackles of bigotry and anti-intellectualism, and if you please, from the indignity of loyalty oaths and unwritten blue laws which no longer apply to other citizens. A teacher, I say, is not a second-class citizen and we must help that profession to regain its erstwhile honor and esteem among us.

National Education Association Convention, Chicago, Illinois, July 6, 1955

Good schools are not cheap. Bad education isn't cheap, either. Its high costs are paid from other budgets — for poverty and sickness, for unemployment and juvenile delinquency. The question is not only, "What will an adequate education program cost?" The question is even more, "What is the cost of not having such a program?" ...

Good school buildings are an asset — but they are not the essence of good teaching education. The real heart of good education remains, as always, good teaching. We must, if we want to improve the quality of education, attract into teaching and hold a far larger number of our ablest young people. Compensation must be geared to ability and performance, and opportunity afforded for advancement to a higher level based on merit, as in other professions.

National Education Association Convention, Chicago, Illinois, July 6, 1955

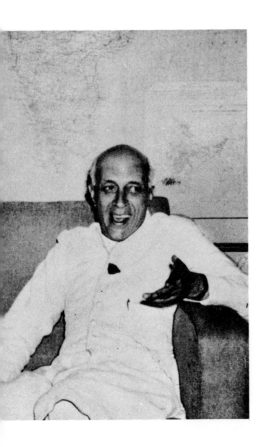

...We must resist the pressures to let mass education become education for mediocrity. The dangers of mass education seem to me as much our problems as are its necessities. . . .

[We must] take very seriously the admonition that education for all may come to mean real education for none. The struggle is very real today between massiveness, standardization, conformity on the one hand, and on the other the spirit of individualism which has given freedom and democracy and life itself meaning.

We must, then, work together to forge better tools for the ever-enlarging job of educating fast growing numbers of our children for an always more complex life. Equally must we strive everlastingly to keep education a process of enrichment —of the mind and spirit of the young American whose destiny is measured only by wisdom.

National Education Association Convention, Chicago, Illinois, July 6, 1955

In growing and changing society, the primary tasks of the school must also grow and change. But we must be clear that if we expect the schools to do too much, if we expect the teacher to play too many roles, we are bound to be disappointed with the results. If our educational purposes are unclear, if the curriculum is chaotic and cluttered with distractions, if the teaching staffs are overburdened with an indiscriminate array of responsibilities well beyond their capacity to carry, we must expect that our children will be educated for mediocrity instead of for something better.

National Education Association Convention, Chicago, Illinois, July 6, 1955

. . . Whatever control of public education is required should be exercised by local authorities. Our public schools take much of their strength from the millions of private citizens who are involved directly in their affairs—the board of trustees, the parent-teachers associations, the room mothers, and all the others. Local control keeps alive continuous debate and the freedom to experiment. It insures a wholesome diversity in educational plans and practices. It helps to keep public education from becoming an instrument of stifling conformity and uniformity. Not sentimental attachment to tradition, but hard-headed good sense demands that by keeping control of education in the local community we keep the spreading of branches of an ever-enlarging democracy always close to its roots.

National Education Association Convention, Chicago, Illinois, July 6, 1955

. . . The teacher's job is to teach the way of inquiry, to prepare each generation to meet its new problems, to improve its new opportunities, to explore civilization's always new horizons, to open minds not to close them.

National Education Association Convention, Chicago, Illinois, July 6, 1955

The victory of peace will come only to the bold and the brave . . .

In a very real sense the central issue of education is the central issue of today: How a civilization which has reached, at least in America, unprecedented heights of material well-being and unlocked awesome secrets of the physical world is also to master the ways for preserving its spiritual and moral and intellectual values — for preserving, if you please, those very things that are the essence of civilization.

. . . For education can serve the ends of democratic society only as it meets those of the individual human being. The essential condition of the system of free choice, which we call democracy, is that it is made up of all different kinds of people and ideas — which means that what we demand most of education is the development of informed people who are at the same time unique, different, unpatterned individuals. I think this means, in turn, that any national educational policy must encourage difference, experimentation and flexibility in educational practice.

National Education Association Convention, Chicago, Illinois, July 6, 1955

It would be the worst of all ironies if we, the richest land in the world, should stand on the sidelines and watch this fateful struggle go against us by default.

In my view, a well considered and carefully administered program of economic and technical assistance to underdeveloped areas should also be a fixed part of the policy of a developed and prosperous country.

Austin, Texas, Sept. 28, 1955

. . . The aim of democratic government is to safeguard the interests, rights and opportunities of all its members, which means to keep a balance between industry, labor, and farmers — to name the three biggest. . . . Whatever the individual good will and virtue of the business leaders, such a concentration of power is dangerous. For government must be the trustee for the little man, because no one else will be. The powerful can usually help themselves — and frequently do. . . .

Democratic Rally, Duluth, Minnesota, Oct. 29, 1955

For the one thing we all are is consumers, and we get the right answers to most of our economic problems by consulting our ultimate interests as consumers.

AFL-CIO Convention, New York, New York, Dec. 8, 1955

...The ultimate goal is not limitation, not an uneasy balance of weapons, or of terror, but the abolition of war by abolition of the means of war. . . .

...It seems to me that the urgency is such that we can settle for nothing less than a sustained and a dogged search for effective disarmament with the best brains we can muster, and that we have no greater foreign policy objective.

University of Virginia, Nov. 11, 1955

Violence is, after all, the confession that mutual relations of respect and goodwill have broken down and the web of common life has been torn apart. The most urgent task before any society, domestic or world-wide, is to check grievances, clashes, blind oppositions of interest, long before they reach the flashpoint of war.

University of Virginia, Nov. 11, 1955

[To say we want to strengthen our way of life] means that we want our children to go to school, not in crowded class-rooms or in basements or on half-day shifts, but in decent build-ings with good teachers proud of their responsibility.

[We] mean that when our children are sick we want them to have decent medical care—and not suffer while the family hesitates because of the doctor's bill.

When they grow old, we want them to have the decent security a life's work entitles them to.

Yes, and the strengthening of our way of life means, too, making more secure the rights of labor to organize and bargain collectively—to make democracy work in the plant, in the shop, on the jobs, in people's daily working lives. The laws must be fair to all, of course: to the workers, to the employer, yes, and to the people, too. . . .

AFL-CIO Convention, New York, New York, Dec. 8, 1955

I came here to summon you . . . to the cause of freedom and to the cause of peace.

And I summon all Americans who believe greatly in these things to join with us. We claim no monopoly on the ideals we assert. They are America's ideals. The victory we seek is not just for a party; it is for a people.

But we do claim that this victory will come only to the bold and to the brave, to those who are willing to work to make democracy's ideals come true in the lives of every man, woman and child in America—yes, and in the world. . . .

We have confidence in ourselves—confidence that we can build what we have to build, that we can grow as we have to grow and that we can change as we must change, and play our full part in the making of a new America—a better tomorrow for ourselves and for all of mankind.

Harrisburg, Pennsylvania, Sept. 13, 1956

Mr. Stevenson entered former President Truman's hotel suite for discussions during the 1956 Democratic convention.

49

Ambassador Stevenson (right) voted on a 1965 U.N. resolution on the Senegal territorial rights question.

Francis Plimpton, deputy U.S. delegate, and Ambassador Stevenson listened to a U.N. debate.

But whoever says that we have arrived at our goal, that this is the best of all possible worlds, convicts himself of the twin sins of complacency and ignorance. He must know very little about the unsatisfied wants — and about the dreams — of human beings. He must know little and care less.

Why we've only just begun to live! And anybody who tells us we've already reached our promised land better get out of the way because if he doesn't he's going to get run over.

Our greatest hope, our most consuming aspiration, is of course for peace, for peace with freedom, without which there can be no tolerable peace.

In the long run the issue between Communism and democracy is going to be finally settled not in the counsels of diplomats or heads of government, but in the hearts and minds — yes, and in the stomachs — of the multitudes of the ordinary working people of Asia, of Africa, of Europe, yes, and of the Americas.

AFL-CIO Convention, New York, New York, Dec. 8, 1955

Men come together in cities," Aristotle said, "in order to live. They remain together in order to live a good life." Yet, twenty-three centuries later, Lewis Mumford's verdict is a good deal less encouraging. "Layer upon layer," he writes, "of past times preserve themselves in the city until life itself is finally threatened with suffocation; then, in sheer defense, modern man invents the museum." "Civilization," he has said elsewhere, critically I think, "is citification."

If civilization is the triumph of science, it is the streamlining of living, if it is material achievement — then, certainly, civilization flourishes today in American cities. . . .

In the external view the first characteristic of our cities is growth; they are growing taller and wider, thrusting across their old boundaries in all directions. Indeed, the button-busting growth of our cities and towns has become the dominant characteristic of our national life, as it is also the companion of industrialism everywhere in the world.

American Municipal Association Convention, Miami, Florida, Nov. 30, 1955

To meet the challenge of the twentieth century we need every resource of imagination, of intelligence, of courage and of faith.

Denver, Colorado, Sept. 22, 1956

. . . Leadership in a democracy can be no more than the capturing of a people's will and the channelling of people's power to realize their own best ideals. I believe so strongly in what I have said here tonight [on a Federal Program for Education] that it makes me uncomfortable that there is nothing any one man can do about it alone.

TV Address on a Federal Program for Education, Milwaukee, Wisconsin, Sept. 28, 1956

My friends, we must place our nation where it belongs in the eyes of the world—at the head of the struggle for peace. For in this nuclear age peace is no longer a visionary ideal. It has become an absolute, imperative, practical necessity. Humanity's long struggle against war has to be won now. Yes, and I say that it can be won.

Chicago, Illinois, Aug. 17, 1956

The United States deplores any war, cold or otherwise. Its only desire is to live in peace and freedom and to let all other peoples live in peace and freedom. It will resist with all of its power all assaults on its own peace and freedom, and it proposes to join with all other peace-loving peoples in resisting in the cooperative framework of the United Nations, all assaults on the peace and freedom of other people. . . .

UN debate on the Congo, New York, New York, Feb. 15, 1961

. . . We must all beware of the resolution which invokes high principle in support of unrealistic action and does nothing to advance a practical solution. If this becomes common practice, we would risk destroying the influence of our organization [U.N.]—for the value of its recommendations would depreciate like inflated currency.

UN General Session, New York, New York, Sept. 20, 1962

Radhakrishna Ramani of Malaysia (left), Stevenson and Lucio Garcia Del Solar of Argentina conferred on the Senegal complaint.

Ambassador Stevenson and U.N. Secretary General U Thant first met in Burma in 1953; later at the U.N. they became close friends.

Communism per se, I am convinced, is not naturally attractive to the bulk of Latin Americans, not even to the many intellectuals who seem most inclined toward it. It is, nevertheless, a magnet that attracts and will continue to draw unhappy people as long as the spokesmen of other political philosophies seem capable only of talk, and can point to no action to right wrongs.

New York, New York, Aug. 5, 1961

Victory of calculated risk over Russian roulette.

Victory of firmness and maturity over the reckless rigidities of know-nothings.

And finally, the victory of cool reason over hot air.

These are the victories that summon a great free nation. In pursuing them, our generation and the next, and the next, will be tested and exasperated year after year by the stubborn weight of history.

Princeton University, Jan. 9, 1962

*By the purity
of our example
we shall
make freedom
meaningful...*

I want to speak tonight of freedom in America.

There can be no lasting freedom in America unless there is peace in the world. And there will be peace in the world only when we here in America prove that freedom means what we say it means. We must show that freedom is the servant of the poor as well as the rich — for most of the world is poor — that it protects change — for most of the world is in revolution — that it is color-blind — for humanity knows no color lines. We must prove that freedom contains that full measure of justice without which it could be freedom for the strong to oppress the weak.

I see freedom in the world today as the great life-giving river of which America is the source. It will be whatever we are, not more, not less. So if we hope to make the principles of freedom meaningful in the world, we must first make sure they have mighty meaning for ourselves. We must — in our land, in our own communities, and in our own hearts — live up to the values of individual freedom and individual right which are the basis of our American society.

Yet we must do this not just because it may exalt our leadership in the world, but, above all, for the sake of these values themselves — the values which give life and power to the great experiment in self-government to which we as a people have been so long committed, and to which so many others in Asia and Africa now urgently aspire. Our task is all the harder and the purity of our example all the more important because these people know little about these values of individual freedom and rights which are at the root of free society. . . .

Only by such a rekindling of this nation's passion for freedom can we persuade the world that America is genuinely the hope of free peoples everywhere. For in the end, democracy will triumph or it will go down, and America will stand or fall, not by the power of our money or of our arms, but by the splendor of our ideals.

New York, New York, April 25, 1956

We know as the world knows that the winds-of-change are blowing all over the world. But the winds-of-change are man-made and man can and must control them. They must not be allowed to become the bugles of war. . . .

The fabric of peace is fragile and our peace-making machinery has today suffered another blow. If it is to survive, if the United Nations is not to die an ignoble death as the League of Nations, we cannot condone the use of force in this instance and thus pave the way for forceful solutions of other disputes which exist in Latin America, Africa, Asia and Europe. In a world as interdependent as ours, the possible results of such a trend are too grievous to contemplate. . . .

At the recess of the 16th session of the UN General Assembly,
New York, New York, Dec. 21, 1961

We are caught up today, along with the rest of the world, in an arms race that threatens mankind with a stark, merciless, and bleak catastrophe.

It is no accident that the instinct of survival which is common to all men and to all nations is slowly but surely compelling the most practical and hard-headed statesmen to give increasing heed to the prevention and abolition of war. In this nuclear age peace is no longer merely a visionary ideal, it has become an urgent and practical necessity. . . .

The search for peace will not end, it will begin with the halting of these [hydrogen bomb] tests. What we will accomplish is a new beginning and the world needs nothing more than a new beginning.

People everywhere, I think, are waiting for the United States to take once more the leadership for peace and for civilization.

We must regain the moral respect that we once had which our stubborn, self-righteous rigidity has nearly lost us.

And finally, I would say to you that leaders must lead; that where the issue is of such magnitude, I have no right to stand silent. I owe it to you to express my views whatever the consequences may be.

I repeat: that this step can be taken. We can break the deadlock. We can make a fresh start. We can put the world on a new path towards peace.

May He who rules us all give us the wisdom and the patience, the courage and the humility which we will need, and grant His blessing to this great work.

TV Address, Chicago, Illinois, Oct. 15, 1956

Over the centuries scores of great men have laid down a mosaic of ethical concepts treating with almost every aspect of human life. Yet, strangely enough, in 1961 millions of persons the world over appear to be groping for new ethical guide lines as if they had never before been traced, or as if the old ones were no longer relevant. . . .

. . . War is no longer rational, we say, yet the response to our mistrust of one another is more lethal weapons. And then we loudly proclaim that we never plan to use them.

It is no wonder that this is the anxious age and that we want an ethic — an ethic for survival. . . .

New York, New York, June 6, 1961

It is the educator, not the engineer, not the businessmen, not the union official, not the bureaucrat, who must tell us how to keep our youngsters in school to prepare them for a productive life.

New School for Social Research, New York,
New York, April 28, 1964

We cannot know where the bugles may blow tomorrow...

After a U.N. meeting, Stevenson explained his views to France's Roger Seydoux.

The United Nations draws its true strength from the sense of solidarity, of common interest, common values, and common ground among the vast majority of its members, quite regardless of regions, races, or blocs. . . .

The central purpose of this body is to keep the peace.

Peace is unstable in many parts of the world, and for many reasons. We live in a world threatened by major war, limited war and brush war. We live in a world of conflicting ideologies and conflicting interests and conflicting purposes. We have inherited the disputes of the centuries. There are danger spots in almost every major area of this planet.

Under the circumstances, it is impossible to predict what new crisis will demand our attention next. It is good news that we have just passed from violence to negotiation in the Congo. We hope against hope for restraint in Berlin. We are entitled to a cautious optimism about the future order of the Southeast Asian peninsula.

But storm flags are up in other places. We cannot know where the bugles may blow tomorrow.

Beyond this, it is painfully evident that pious platitudes do not keep the peace — nor verbal respect for great principles — nor does sterile debate. It is painfully evident that the rule of law and order requires the means for enforcing the law — that peaceful change and the settlement of disputes require machinery for effecting change and containing dispute.

And it is painfully evident that we have neither used as well as we might the existing procedures for peaceful settlements and the peace keeping machinery of the United Nations, nor have we used them frequently enough.

At the recess of the 16th session of the UN General Assembly,
New York, New York, Dec. 21, 1961

In the great struggle to advance civil and human rights even a jail sentence is no longer a dishonor but a proud achievement.

Perhaps we are destined to see in this law-loving land people running for office not on their stainless records but on their prison records.

The slums and tenements, the poor schools, the joblessness — this is the great unfinished business which the civil rights bill does not remedy.

The lesson for all of us, therefore, is: fight against injustice and for its victims, yes; but cure the miseries through homes and cities and schools and work places good enough for all.

Colby College, Waterville, Maine, June 7, 1964

...A nation is not created by a stroke of a pen. A declaration of political independence is a beginning not a conclusion. Nothing more discredits the great historic transformation of our epoch than for newly independent states to fall into chaos and become an international problem or an international danger. The long labor of nationhood requires the reality as well as the rhetoric of independence: it requires an emerging national will capable of the political wisdom, the administrative vigor, the economic energy and the moral discipline necessary to convert the promise of national independence into a free and productive life for its people. The interest of my government and of the world lies not in the mere multiplication of nations —but in the multiplication of nations where peoples are free and have the strength to survive, and to grow and to contribute to the vitality of the international order in the world community.

UN General Session, New York, New York, Sept. 20, 1962

As ambassador to the U.N.,
Stevenson faced anti-U.N. demonstrators
in Dallas, Texas, shortly before
President Kennedy's assassination.

If the United Nations has not succeeded in bringing the great powers together, it has often succeeded in keeping them apart—in places where face-to-face confrontation might have changed difficult situations into impossible situations.

UN General Session, New York, New York, Sept. 20, 1962

It becomes increasingly difficult . . . to understand the logic of these super-patriots who decry the United Nations; who talk of peace but who object to our only institution for peaceful settlement; who decry every attempt at negotiation and conciliation and offer no alternative save weapons that will destroy friend and foe alike.

The big question we face today, of course, is whether the Communist bloc will ever look in the same direction as we do. The answer may be a long time in coming.

But the recently concluded nuclear test-ban treaty, now signed by more than 100 countries, is the most important single step taken since the war in the field of arms control and disarmament.

Dallas, Texas, Oct. 24, 1963

Change is the remorseless master of us all. . . .

The image of the automation engineer may not excite the imagination as does the image of the astronaut, but the fate of mankind in the forseeable future will depend more on what we do manipulating machines here on earth than how we do hurtling them through the heavens.

. . . There is no longer any retreat into cozy compartmentalized thinking in which domestic problems are neatly sorted, sanitized and wrapped to be opened, served and solved domestically one at a time.

New School for Social Research, New York,
New York, April 28, 1964

57

Stevenson told students at Northwestern University that ". . . knowledge gives . . . freedom from prejudice and ignorance."

*T*olerance through understanding, steadiness in truth; these are the fruits of education . . .

The objective of peace is inseparably intertwined with the objective of progress.

UN General Session, New York, New York, Sept. 20, 1962

The right we seek to defend is the right of people, be it in Korea or South Vietnam, not to have their future decided by violence.

I do not believe this right can be secured by retreat. Retreat leads to retreat, just as aggression leads to aggression in this still primitive international community.

Harvard University, June 17, 1965

All of us know the moving claim that "the truth shall make you free," but I wonder how often we take the trouble to look a little more clearly at its meaning. In the first place, knowledge, learning, access to the facts are a precondition of free and responsible government. So long as learning is locked up in a small minority, the mass of the people lack the information and hence the courage to act. All traditional societies are based on learning confined to the elite; free, open society rests on the knowledge of the many. As free men we are not oppressed by mysteries and secrets. We can judge and act because we can observe and know.

Then again knowledge gives us freedom from prejudice and ignorance which tyranny so often manipulates to its own ends. . . . The man who knows nothing about society or his neighbor or history or basic economic and social realities falls into the world of devils and dreams. If he cannot explain happenings which he finds difficult, he falls back on the magic of supposed spite and ill will.

In any society, there are interests that clash, difficulties that have to be confronted. Faced in ignorance, they will be settled in prejudice and fear. But if their causes are grasped and the compulsions behind them understood, a saving tolerance and compassion, a fruitful reference to fact and reason, can create the context in which deadlocks are avoided and compromises reached which point to the way ahead.

. . . An open society must rely on the confidence and good faith of its citizens, on their readiness to work together in friendship and trust. But a society riddled with ignorance and prejudice does not produce such a confidence in the integrity of others. . . . And if all this has been true in the past — largely within the confines of our great Republic — how much more true is it of our future? The universities have been our bulwark against the risks of prejudice and hostility in a society made up of every culture, faith and race. They have taught us the tolerance bred of understanding, the steadiness born of truth.

But now we face a whole planetary society in which the differences are greater still, but our involvement hardly less. Once again, in the new world order, which science and technology thrust irresistibly upon us, the universities are called to raise the torch of truth and learning that alone can light the difficult paths toward our goal of freedom. . . . The challenge is not different from the challenge of the past, but it is incomparably greater.

. . . American universities are called to play a new part beyond these shores. Cooperating with new centers of learning, receiving foreign scholars, lending teachers, creating new relations with institutions overseas, they have to find new ways in which the freedom born of the knowledge which we enjoy here in America can be achieved in other lands.

Northwestern University, Oct. 7, 1964

President Kennedy and
Ambassador Stevenson shared common views
on the necessity of United States
support for the United Nations.

In mid-1952, Governor Stevenson and Vice President Alben Barkley talked to Trygve Lie, U.N. Secretary General.

In the years since I left the Law School of this great University, in barely half a man's lifetime, we have been pitched from isolation to a world so small that a pushbutton can blow it up. We have been drawn from a state of virtually no concern with our neighbors to one of perpetual, daily, hourly responsibility. And perhaps "responsibility" is hardly an adequate word. For, to me, it still carries too great a sense of choice, of voluntary action. Some of today's political oratory sounds as if we had a choice, that we could condescendingly step in and help the less competent and powerful peoples — or that we could rattle our rockets and intimidate the "bad guys" — or act as a benevolent, but still detached, protector of public order and patron of the poor.

But it is not like that at all. We are not Roman emperors. We are not the grand Khans of Tartary. We are not well-meaning philanthropists or lady bountifuls. We are like everybody else — poor benighted members of the ship's company, exposed to the same risks of death and destruction, depending for survival on the same thin soil, vulnerable to all the common hazards of humanity — from tornadoes to power-drunk dictators.

We can't choose to help or not to help. We can't patronize. We can't coerce. And we can't drop out. We are all in it together, we, the human race . . . and we either learn, all of us, to do a better job of running [this planet earth] or we shall all perish together. For, in the nuclear age, there is nowhere else to go. At least, not yet!

Northwestern University, Oct. 7, 1964

We the human race cannot live as strangers...

[I wasn't concerned about protests on the nation's campuses] probably because I have been picketed, applauded and abused everywhere from Texas to Toronto.

American University, Washington, D. C., June 13, 1965

We can re-examine the terms of our alliance, but surely the world is not yet so safe that anyone can afford to break it up.

We face in Communist hostility and expansionism a formidable force whether Mr. Khrushchev and Mr. Mao Tse-tung pull together or apart.

Their disagreement so far only turns on the point whether capitalism should be peacefully or violently buried. They are both for the funeral.

It cannot be patriotism to enlarge a country's illusory sense of potency and influence and reduce its security and economic viability.

True patriotism demands that in some essential categories purely national solutions be left behind in the interest of the nation itself.

On this shrunken globe men can no longer live as strangers. Men can war against each other as hostile neighbors, as we are determined not to do; or they can co-exist in frigid isolation, as we are doing.

But our prayer is that men everywhere will learn, finally to live as brothers, to respect each other's differences, to heal each other's wounds, to promote each other's progress, and to benefit from each other's knowledge.

Our basic reason for being a state is our attempt to build a dynamic and equal society of free men.

But if the world's first experiment in the open society uses patriotism as a cloak for inaction or reaction, then it will cease to open and then, as a social organism, it will lose its fundamental reason for existence. . . .

It is only if keen and lively minds constantly compare the ideal and the reality and see the shadow — the shadow of self-righteousness, the shadow of slums and poverty, the shadow of delinquent children, the shadow of suburban sprawls, the shadow of racial discrimination, the shadow of interminable strikes — it is only then that shadows can be dispelled and the unique brightness of our national experiment can be seen and loved.

South Bend, Indiana, Feb. 18, 1963

Through the United Nations, Stevenson believed world unity was possible.

61

Stevenson was committed to people; to the individual and all humanity.

III

Stevenson
and the American People

Many a reporter, even those with many opportunities to observe, has written of Adlai Stevenson as a shy, solitary man, whose distaste for crowds was a major political liability. But anyone who thinks that people of any kind, or in any quantity, did not interest him is wrong. His commitment to people was revealed in many ways. For example, in his speeches and the care he lavished on them.

The word "orator" is today surrounded by some of the flavor that attends "buffoon, charlatan, mountebank, demagogue," or — in places where the oration is appreciated—the word is washed with the over-sweet perfume of "anachronism." The word "speech" evokes an image of genial, unrehearsed, ghost-written, all-purpose, glib, easily forgettable interludes incorporated into many of the folk rituals of our society.

That Mr. Stevenson's public utterance was none of these things is known by everyone who ever heard, or read, or read about him. But what is perhaps not as often mentioned is that he was, not only determined to say precisely what he wanted to say, but he also knew that he had to trick his audience into listening. He knew— as some men of artless goodwill do not—that in communicating, the test of success is not what the speaker means to say, but rather what the listener thinks he has heard.

Everyone agrees that Mr. Stevenson was a master speaker, but it is not always easy to understand what goes into such mastery. Some who are qualified to understand such matters have said they would have voted for Mr. Stevenson if for no other reason than simply because of the way he wrote, rewrote, revised and polished his speeches up to the moment of their delivery. His speeches were not written in a vacuum, nor for a lamp-lit library. He spoke to his audience; and if, after it became apparent that he would never have patronage to distribute, some audiences did not give him their complete attention it was because what he was trying to say was difficult to say, and not just a verification of his listeners' prejudices.

In fact, his greatest virtue was, in a sense, his greatest obstacle in communicating with a crowd. He talked to people, rather than to *the* people. Many a politician is more at ease talking to a rally of friendly strangers than in chatting with a few of his friends. Many a socially conscious activist is happier helping a distant down-trodden humanity than in meeting a slum dweller face to face. These people are like tourists, charmed with the distant beauty of orchards, who aren't interested in the kind of trees that grow there, and who would hate to examine the leaves. Mr. Stevenson admired the view as much as anyone, but he also had a well-developed taste for the fruit.

Mr. Stevenson was interested in people the way a book collector is interested in rare first editions. Everyone he met was different, and he was concerned with, and charmed by, their difference. This could be seen as he stood in receiving lines, giving his full attention, along with his hand, to each of the nameless faithful.

When he spoke of *mankind* he did not think of an abstraction, or a word chalked on a blackboard for discussion, or a philosophical-demographic generality. It was as if the word "mankind" (and all its synonyms, and all the concepts related to it) flashed before his imagination a sweeping splendid panorama of individuals which—it was his special gift—he saw in their specifically unique, and to him beautiful, differences.

It was not because crowds interested him less than individuals that some people thought he was uneasy in their presence; it was because they interested him more because they contained more individuals. A crowd was to him what a table of assorted candies is to a child: he wanted to sample each piece of it, all at once.

Adlai Stevenson was the admired confidant of many of his great contemporaries. It is remarkable how many of them spoke of him with pride as their friend, and how often he himself used the word "friend," with overtones of affection, in all of his speeches. Writing after the campaign of 1952 he said that meeting the electorate was "a glorious, heart-filling, odyssey" for which he would be forever grateful, and that the great masses of his fellow Americans whom he had seen and talked to would be remembered always. "Their faces," he wrote, "are a friendly, smiling sea of memory stretching from coast to coast." And that seems to sum up a significant part of Adlai Stevenson: his sometimes unrequited love for the American people and all people.

I believe any citizen should make whatever contribution he can to search for a safer, saner world.

. . . Our prosperity and wealth can now be used to give all of our people the higher standards and wider opportunities which are mankind's universal dream. These are now within our reach, not simply for the favored few, but for every family in America.

Chicago, Illinois, Nov. 15, 1955

A democratic society can't stand still, and the world in which we live won't stand still. Both are living things and the meaning of life is in growth, in working always toward something better, toward something higher. Moderation, yes. But stagnation, no! As the history of the rise and fall of nations before us reminds us, nothing fails like success.

Democratic Dinner, Chicago, Illinois, Nov. 19, 1955

You know, there are at least two reasons why it is difficult to run for President. One of them is that you always have to speak last after everything has been said. And another is that you have to shave twice a day.

Speech to the Liberal Party, New York, New York, Sept. 11, 1956

President Johnson has directed me to affirm to this Assembly that there will be no "Johnson policy" toward the United Nations—any more than there was a "Kennedy policy." There was—and is—only a United States policy, and that too outlasts violence and outlives men.

UN, New York, New York, Nov. 26, 1963

At the 1960 Democratic convention, Presidential hopefuls John F. Kennedy, Stevenson and Lyndon B. Johnson shook hands.

We must meet the challenges of our times, for humanity is above all nations...

Poverty in Latin America was observed by Stevenson when he toured Lima, Peru.

The hearts of the American people go out to the people of Europe and we share to the full the faith that has been expressed here in the restoration of Europe both in body and spirit, to her exalted place in the advancing of civilization of the world and in the cause of peace. Location of the headquarters of the United Nations in the United States must not mean that the United Nations will now or ever turn its back upon Europe. On the contrary.

On the location of the UN in the United States,
New York, New York, Dec. 15, 1945

We both believe in diversity, but the things that bind us together from our common poetry to our nursery rhymes and the language of our prayers, are far more important than elocution and protestations of good will. There is nothing fundamentally wrong with the relations between Britain and the U.S. . . . ,

New York, New York, Aug. 20, 1953

. . . Don't be afraid to learn, to read, to study, to try to know. . . .

And don't be afraid to live, to live hard and fast.

Princeton University, March 22, 1954

We want to do nothing through Government which can be done privately, but private industry and Government together must do whatever is necessary to meet democracy's and free capitalism's essential goal.

Government must shape its policies, too, so as to encourage in every conceivable way this process of private expansion and growth. The one sure-fire incentive for any industry is customers.

The function of democratic capitalism is not just making things; the system works only as it gets the things it makes into the lives of people who can use them. So my own belief is that in the present situation the emphasis should be on encouraging consumption.

Charlotte, North Carolina, April 2, 1954

Even now there are many Americans who don't yet have enough to eat or a properly balanced diet. And if other countries could earn the dollars to buy the food they want and need there would be no farm surplus problem in America. For throughout this teeming, troubled, growing world two in every three persons are slowly starving to death.

The fact is there is no surplus of food in the world; there is a terrible shortage. . . .

There cannot be in today's hungry world a surplus of corn or wheat. There can only be a shortage of ideas or a weakness of will to learn how to use God's gifts for His children.

Sioux Falls, South Dakota, Aug. 25; 1954

. . . Methods must be worked out for making medical services better available to all who need them, and without crippling cost to anyone. We are spending more than ten billion dollars a year for medical expenses. We are willing, if we have to, to pay more. But we want to make this expenditure as effective as possible, to realize the economy of preventive medicine, to assure the distribution of medical service on a basis of need for it, and to remove the haunting fear in so many American homes that if serious sickness strikes it will wipe out every cent of savings, perhaps cut off all earning power, and destroy life's dignity even if life itself is spared.

. . . In too many American homes a parent at sometime or other looks down at a sick child, knows that something should be done and that there isn't the money to do it.

Bellevue Medical Center, New York, New York, June 2, 1955

. . . It is not to increase the national income that we seek to stop needless sickness and death. It is in terms not of dollars but of humanity that the case for medical research is to be made. And we want to be led toward health even as toward prosperity and peace. We have answered willingly, and often, leadership's call for crash programs to build better instruments of death. And now we ask humbly for leadership — from the profession and the government — for programs to build better instruments of life. We seek, together as a people, freedom — including the freedom to live.

Bellevue Medical Center, New York, New York, June 2, 1955

As Woodrow Wilson devised new methods to promote the common good among men and peace among nations, so must we devise new methods to meet the challenges of our times. Surely this is what the spirit of Wilson has to say to us today. . . . It is the spirit that justice transcends victory, that "humanity is above all nations," "that every man beareth the stamp of the human conditions." . . .

University of Virginia, Nov. 11, 1955

1956 Democratic nominee Stevenson joined former President Truman for an early morning walk.

Governor Stevenson toured the Lawrenceville, Illinois, flood area in 1950 during rescue operations.

. . . The farm problem . . . the conservation problem, the education problem, the minorities problem, the great and overriding problem of our national survival. . . .

Each of these problems breaks down into the reflection of the life and times of human beings—of . . . farmers in Minnesota, and factory workers in New Jersey, and fishermen in Maine, and orange pickers in California, and cotton choppers in Georgia. . . . Our eternal concern [is] with the way men live, and the way men dream, and with the opportunity each must have to take his rightful place in the long march of history.

Democratic Rally, Duluth, Minnesota, Oct. 29, 1955

. . . Enterprise depends upon opportunity—opportunity for a man with talent, with energy to branch out on his own—to build his own business, own his own plant, take his own risks, make his own decisions. . . .

Woodrow Wilson put it in these words: "I understand it to be the fundamental proposition of American liberty that we do not desire special privilege because we know special privilege will never comprehend the general welfare. . . ."

. . . Democracy serves no one except as it serves us all.

Democratic Dinner, Chicago, Illinois, Nov. 19, 1955

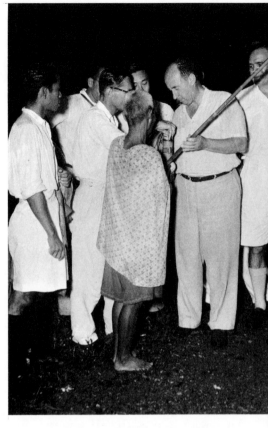

While in Southeast Asia, Stevenson received a blowgun from Malaysian natives.

At the Illinois State Fairgrounds in Springfield, Governor Stevenson (center) and Lieutenant Governor Sherwood Dixon (far right) led veterans' organization leaders in Veterans' Day ceremonies.

Democracy serves all or serves no one . . .

Miners rescued from a mine disaster near Springfield, Illinois, were met by Governor Stevenson.

Stevenson, Britain's Sir Patrick Dean and Ellis Clarke of Trinidad and Tobago conversed at the U.N.

W̲e mean by "politics," the people's business — the most important business there is.

We mean the conduct of the people's business by all of the people, in open meetings where we can say what we think, and what we think should be done — about what we think!

Democratic Dinner, Chicago, Illinois, Nov. 19, 1955

W̲e must make the world understand again what it once knew so well — that at the roots of our American faith we recognize that we belong, all of us, to the family of man.

Democratic Dinner, Chicago, Illinois, Nov. 19, 1955

I̲n each of these traditions, systems of sanctions, and dialects of morals, there is a residue of what might be called wisdom. Much of what is done in the name of this wisdom may seem to us of another world utter folly, just as no doubt much of what we do must seem bizarre to peoples of other backgrounds.

New York, New York, June 6, 1961

C̲ontemplating this completed career, we feel a sense of enlargement and exhilaration. Like the grandeur and power of the masterpieces of art and music, Churchill's life uplifts our hearts and fills us with fresh revelation of the scale and reach of human achievement. We may be sad; but we rejoice as well, as all must rejoice when they "now praise famous men" and see in their lives the full splendor of our human estate.

. . . In the last analysis all the zest and life and confidence of this incomparable man sprang, I believe, not only from the rich endowment of his nature but also from a profound and simple faith in God.

In the prime of his powers, confronted with the apocalyptic risks of annihilation, he said serenely: "I do not believe that God has despaired of His children."

We shall hear no longer the remembered eloquence and wit, the old courage and defiance, the robust serenity of indomitable faith. Our world is thus poorer, our political dialogue is diminished and the sources of public inspiration run more thinly for all of us. There is a lonesome place against the sky.

Eulogy in Washington Cathedral for Sir Winston S. Churchill, Washington, D. C., Jan. 28, 1965

Western society is the first in which all men can expect an equal chance...

While in Malaya, Stevenson watched British soldiers return from jungle patrol.

A Kenyan woman's native costume was admired by Stevenson.

... In the face of all that has happened in the Congo, we hope that men of goodwill will everywhere join together with sober resolve not to seek revenge but to seek reconciliation.

To the UN on the death of Patrice Lumumba, Feb. 13, 1961

I know there is much dissatisfaction about aid, much feeling that it is wasted and never achieves a "breakthrough," and dribbles away down thousands of unspecified drains and ratholes. Yet just so did the Victorians talk about tax money devoted to lifting the standards of the very poor in early industrial society. There were the "good poor" who said "please" and "thank you" and touched their forelocks. Then there were the "bad poor" who kept coal in a bath tub. But over a couple [of] generations, it was the raising of all this unfortunate mass of humanity that turned Western society into the first social order in history in which everyone would expect something of an equal chance.

After ten years, we are only at the beginning of the experiment of international aid. We are learning greatly. We see the relevance of some policies, the supreme obstacles offered by others. We discriminate more. We are learning to be better givers. . . .

Convention of the Center for the Study of Democratic Institutions, New York, New York, Jan. 22, 1963

Like so many others I have lost more than a beloved friend. I have lost an inspiration. She would rather light a candle than curse the darkness, and her glow has warmed the world.

On the death of Mrs. Eleanor Roosevelt, Nov. 7, 1962

The tragedy of this day is beyond instant comprehension. All of us who knew him will bear the grief of his death to the day of ours. And all men everywhere who love peace and justice and freedom will bow their heads. At such a moment we can only turn to prayer, prayer to comfort our grief, to sustain Mrs. Kennedy and his family, to strengthen President Johnson and to guide us in time to come. May God help us.

On the death of President John F. Kennedy, New York, New York, Nov. 23, 1963

He was a great soldier, an intrepid spirit and gallant gentleman. His courage was as high as the flag his troops raised: "Hoist the colors to its peak and let no enemy haul them down."

On the death of General Douglas MacArthur, April 5, 1964

Stevenson (left) and world leaders
went to Uppsala, Sweden, to the funeral of
U.N. Secretary General Dag Hammarskjold.

Above: Adlai Stevenson (center) and
Senator Estes Kefauver attended church
services during the 1956 campaign.
Above right: In 1964, Stevenson con-
gratulated newly elected U.N. Security
Council President Alex Quaison-Sackey.

Tunisian Foreign Minister
Mongi Slim and Ambassador Stevenson
discussed U.N. policies.

Stevenson conveyed his salient ideas through a combination of meaningful expression and symbolic humor.

IV
The Stevenson Style

Adlai Stevenson entered the area of common conversational recognition as a champion high-stylist of the close-knit intellectual elite. As such, he received about an equal measure of published praise and blame during the summer months of his first Presidential campaign (and some of this reputation improperly remains), but as the serious electioneering of the fall got underway, and as more and more could-be voters heard him speak, his partisans began to use the more "electable" words "thoughtful and reasonable," and his opponents concentrated their critical fire on his humor.

The exclusive label of the withdrawn thinker, as distinct from the man of action, never fitted Adlai Stevenson. His style was, and will continue to be, appreciated in the study and the library, but it was a platform style, a crusader's speech, and (if you will raise the words to their highest sense) it was locker-room oratory before engaging in the violent game called "survival."

One had only to listen to Mr. Stevenson to realize that no one could fault him for exclusiveness of attitude or esoteric thought. His speech was full of reminiscence proper to the group before whom he stood. He seemed to understand, not only the problems of his audience, but also the language they used to formulate those problems.

His vocabulary was filled with color and precision, but there were seldom words that needed to be looked up in order to understand the context of his exposition. It is true that he used the learned specially proper word for some uncommon things, but most of the things he talked about were close enough to everybody to be part of a common heritage and hope and understanding.

At one time it was necessary for Stevenson supporters to attack the attitude of mind that expressed itself something like this: "I understand Governor Stevenson, but he's talking over the heads of everyone else." The defenders of the Governor's style pointed out the fallacy of this position. They pointed out that those who felt people other than themselves couldn't understand a Stevensonian speech were, by the people they looked down upon, often thought to be lacking in the understanding of the same speech.

There may be those who seriously hold the opinion that some normal twentieth-century Americans were incapable of understanding Adlai Stevenson. That such an opinion is correct can be refuted with vigor and scores of illustrative examples.

The difficulty with what Mr. Stevenson said was not in understanding him, but in being willing to accept his ideas. For his ideas were not easy, or comforting, or day-dreaming ideas. His ideas stood away from the props of instinctive selfishness and required backbone from those who stood with them; they were moving ideas that asked for an answering movement to keep pace with them; they were lifting ideas that required an equal surge of muscle from those who were inspired by them.

It was more self-protective to say that the ideas were hard to understand than it was to admit they were hard to accept or act upon. It was also easier. But it wasn't true.

Mr. Stevenson decorated these ideas with wit and humor that was really part of the idea itself. Sometimes this light touch was criticized as reflecting an improper frivolity and lack of concern for the serious business of our times. The most devastating, if uncharitable, answer to such critics is to quote them accurately in the presence of the words they criticize. But almost everyone understood Mr. Stevenson's reasonable assumption that laughter was a good thing, and that it is easier to communicate with people who are listening for a joke than with those soothed into semi-consciousness by the thin air of high-level platitudes.

Mr. Stevenson's wit and humor were not based on satire, or special reference, or in-group situation irony. The laughter he evoked came out of universal appeal and the smiles of his listeners were part of a shared experience and tradition. He laughed with them at common incongruities, except when he laughed at himself.

He was not a teller of pointless funny stories or a maker of misdirected (or undirected) jokes. The anecdote, the pleasantry, the pun, were part of his pleasure in the unexpected, unpredictable, incomprehensible and wonderful thing it is to be a human being. In his formal utterance his wit and humor always served the main purpose of his discourse; it either led directly into his subject or illustrated or explained a point he wanted to make. He used humor, when he used it deliberately, like a trout fisherman uses a hackle tied to his hook.

Informally, his humor grew out of his graciousness. During the tiresome, harried, destructive, distracting moments of politicking, those who continually observed him never saw him lose his sympathy and interest in people as individuals. Everyone who met him, even for a moment, felt that Adlai Stevenson was his special, particular friend. And, in a sense, everyone was right. So the private humor of Mr. Stevenson was always among friends.

Sleepy, tired, hot and ill-fed, he would be dragged into a badly ventilated hall where, chained to a podium or a receiving line or a dinner table, he would be wildly smiled at by local party regulars and handshake-hungry volunteers who had contributed to the campaign. Even when under the savage attack of this bloodthirsty good will, his affection for people never noticeably deserted him and he scattered his humor with a seemingly inexhaustible largesse.

A woman reaches across a table to clutch the hand he is using to pencil revisions on a speech. She says: "I've just been dying to tell you how much I admire you." The candidate looks up, focuses on her, shifts the gears of his attention, and smiles as though the tribute was his most prized possession. He says: "Well, I don't want you to die before you vote, but still I hope meeting me hasn't cured you completely."

The word "style" can mean many things in English. It may refer to the ordered presentation of unique and original thought; it may refer to clothing worn according to a common fashion. But in any sense it is supposed to identify the man who uses it.

The style of Adlai E. Stevenson's writing and speaking (like the style of his living) grew out of his special way of thinking, and feeling, and acting out his warm concern for the great things common to all men. It was indifferent to fad or fashion, but it delighted in the bright, and the good, and the gay, and the true, and the beautiful. It was a style worth imitating, because it was, and did reflect, a great man.

To the honorable, the members of the Senate of the 66th general assembly:

I herewith return, without my approval, Senate bill 93 entitled, "an act to provide protection to insectivorous birds by restraining cats." This is the so-called "cat bill." I veto and withhold my approval from this bill for the following reasons:

It would impose fines on owners or keepers who permitted their cats to run at large off their premises. It would permit any person to capture, or call upon the police to pick up and imprison, cats at large. It would permit the use of traps. The bill would have state-wide application — on farms, in villages, and in metropolitan centers.

This legislation has been introduced in the past several sessions of the legislature, and it has, over the years, been the source of much comment—not all of which has been in a serious vein. It may be that the general assembly has now seen fit to refer it to one who can view it with a fresh outlook. Whatever the reasons for passage at this session, I cannot believe there is a widespread public demand for this law or that it could, as a practical matter, be enforced.

Furthermore, I cannot agree that it should be the declared public policy of Illinois that a cat visiting a neighbor's yard or crossing the highway is a public nuisance. It is in the nature of cats to do a certain amount of unescorted roaming. Many live with their owners in apartments or other restricted premises, and I doubt if we want to make their every brief foray an opportunity for a small game hunt by zealous citizens — with traps or otherwise.

I am afraid this bill could only create discord, recrimination and enmity. Also consider the owner's dilemma: To escort a cat abroad on a leash is against the nature of the cat, and to permit it to venture forth for exercise unattended into a night of new dangers is against the nature of the owner. Moreover, cats perform useful service, particularly in rural areas, in combating rodents — work they necessarily perform alone and without regard for party lines.

We are all interested in protecting certain varieties of birds. That cats destroy some birds, I well know, but I believe this legislation would further but little the worthy cause to which its proponents give such unselfish effort.

The problem of cat versus bird is as old as time. If we attempt to resolve it by legislation, who knows but what we may be called upon to take sides as well in the age old problems of dog versus cat, bird versus bird, or even bird versus worm. In my opinion, the state of Illinois and its local governing bodies already have enough to do without trying to control feline delinquency.

For these reasons, and not because I love birds the less or cats the more, I veto and withhold my approval from Senate bill No. 93.

Governor's Message, Springfield, Illinois, April 23, 1949

Libertyville, Illinois, Stevenson's hometown, welcomed visitors with this sign.

I am about to leave you on a long journey...

I'm deeply moved by what has taken place tonight and I have never been more conscious of the appalling responsibilities of the office. I did not seek it. I did not want it.

I am, however, persuaded that to shirk it, to evade, to decline, would be to repay honor with dishonor.

I shall go now to the convention hall and accept the nomination of the Democratic party.

My party reached its decision openly and fairly. It has asked of me nothing except that I give such poor talents as I have to the service of my country. That I will do and gladly on behalf of the millions for whom my party speaks; and I hope on behalf of millions more. I feel no exultation and no sense of triumph whatever; nothing but humbleness and humility.

And like all of us in need, I shall ask my God to nourish my spirit and to give me the strength and the courage for this great undertaking in the great hour of history.

Front Porch Speech, Chicago, Illinois, July 26, 1952

And now I must go away in quest of an even greater office, and leave behind not only you, my friends, but also my work here in Springfield.

It is not easy to say farewell to you or to that work which has been my total life. For all the sweat and tears I have been richly rewarded.

I am about to leave you on a long journey, and the route, by the way, won't be a military secret. I intend to cover as much ground as time and strength and resources permit. And I won't call it a "crusade" to exterminate Republicans. I like a lot of Republicans, even some very new converts to that faith, whatever it is. Indeed, there are some Republicans I would trust with anything—anything, that is, except public office. No, my journey won't be a crusade: we'll just call it Operation Victory.

Illinois State Fair, Springfield, Illinois, Aug. 14, 1952

We say that every American boy has a chance to be President when he grows up—and I've concluded that that's just one of the risks he takes!

Democratic Rally, Neptune, New Jersey, Aug. 27, 1952

Incidentally, I had been under the very distinct impression, a few months back, that the Republicans had made off with the Democratic farm plank. I guess I was wrong. They just borrowed it temporarily, and returned it very early in November.

Democratic Dinner, Los Angeles, California, Feb. 26, 1953

You know how it is in an election year they pick a President and then for four years they pick on him. . . .

I've been much interested, in the continued debate that's been raging in the newspapers as to whether I was headed right, center, or left. I think it would have been rather more relevant had they asked: Is the man moving forward, backward, or is he grounded.

Now I sometimes think we're far more tolerant of a quarterback than we are of our candidates. An advance on the football field through left guard, or through right guard, or even straight through center, is generally counted as yardage gained. I think it's the sports writer's word for it. The only unforgiving thing is to be trapped by the Old Guard behind your line. Whatever may happen, I trust that it will be said of me that I know the difference between the goal line and the side line.

Speech to Liberal Party, New York, New York, Aug. 28, 1952

At his Illinois farm, Stevenson enjoyed hours of quiet relaxation.

If the best hope for today's world is a kind of atomic balance, the decisive battle in the struggle against aggression may be fought not on battlefields but in the minds of men, and the area of decision may well be out there among the uncommitted peoples of Asia and of Africa who look and listen and who must in the main, judge us by what we say and do. . . .

I am a great believer in national humility, modesty, self-examination and self-criticism, and I have preached these virtues vigorously, although, of course, I haven't practiced them. . . .

There are rising voices here and abroad that forget that although America occasionally gags on a gnat, it also has some talent for swallowing tigers whole: voices that tell us our national energy is spent, that our old values have decayed, that it is futile to try to restore them.

There are voices that say that at best we are as Rome; that once our bridges, our skyscrapers, our factories and our weapons fall before the iron law of decay, no traces will be left—no great issues, no great cause to mark our past universal history.

And there are voices that seem to say that we are as Carthage, that our vital principle is commerce, just commerce; our ethics, our politics, our imaginative faculties, they say, are all bent and twisted to serve our sovereign—commerce.

Other voices cry havoc, fear that America is not equal to the task; that Communism is the way to the future—is irresistible, just as Fascism was for them not so long ago.

Even novelists and poets seem to have been infected. Humanism passes as realism. The very excitement in a time of change and testing is suspect.

I don't know, but I do know that if we doubt ourselves we will persuade no one. If we doubt our mission in the world, we will do nothing to advance it. . . .

Columbia University, June 5, 1954

Stevenson, who liked rural
life in the Midwest,
with his son, John Fell (below).

Democracy must grow
to live . . .

But the great fault will not be in falling short. The fault will be in not seeing that there is a higher goal, that democracy's star moves in the orbit of mankind's growth—never to be reached but to be forever pursued. Democracy's leadership must look for its guidance at that star—not to last year's statistics. For we will live only as we grow.

Democratic Rally, Minneapolis, Minnesota, Sept. 25, 1954

"Let us," in Thomas Jefferson's words, "restore to social intercourse that harmony and affection without which liberty and even life itself are dreary things," and without which, I could add, tomorrow's misfortunes will mock today's expectations.

Southern Democratic Conference, Miami Beach, Florida, March 6, 1954

You can have all the productive capacity in the world; but it doesn't seem to help business if business doesn't have buyers. The best business stimulant at a time like this is customers walking in the front door with money in their pants.

Charlotte, North Carolina, April 2, 1954

We have as a people—in our soil and rivers, and in our hands and our genius and our hearts—every asset we need to create a fuller life for every American in every year of our fore-seeable future.

Charlotte, North Carolina, April 2, 1954

We cannot stand still. We must go forward to stay in the same place—and very much forward if we want to achieve the progress the American people demand.

Charlotte, North Carolina, April 2, 1954

But taxes and tariffs are in a sense details. The under-lying question is whether it is to be the basic policy of this country to use its full resources or only part of them. It is the question, in terms of the parable, whether we are going to bury our talents or whether we intend to use them to the full so that they may be returned twice over to our Master through our fuller lives as His children. It is the question, basically, of faith and courage.

Charlotte, North Carolina, April 2, 1954

The Stevenson family farm heritage extended from Stevenson's pioneer ancestors. He spent much leisure time at his Libertyville home (right and below).

A year ago many newspapers . . . were saying that the Republicans must be elected to save the Grand Old Party from destroying itself . . . that given office they would measure up to the responsibility, somehow heal their divisions, reduce taxes, balance the budget, cut waste, cut military expenditures, strengthen the free world, liberate the enslaved, restore peace and light, milk and manna to the world.

Well, that would have been about as easy as for one Siamese twin to jump off Brooklyn Bridge while the other kept the skillet hot for the fish fry. And today the gulf between their promises and their performances is as wide as Texas.

Georgia Legislature, Nov. 24, 1953

For the university is the archive of the Western mind, it's the keeper of the Western culture, and the foundation of Western culture is freedom. Men may be born free; they cannot be born wise; and it is the duty of the university to make the free wise. The university is the guardian of our heritage, the teacher of our teachers. It's the dwelling place of the free mind.

Columbia University, June 5, 1954

I venture to say that there are in the world many with a deep, intense longing for a vision of a better life not in a material, but in a spiritual sense; for love, for human solidarity. There is a hunger to hear a word of truth, a longing for an ideal, a readiness for sacrifice. . . .

And I think that deep down the ideas of independence, of individuality, of free initiative, represent the strongest appeals to Americans who want to think for themselves, who don't want to be creatures of mass suggestion, who don't want to be automations.

Columbia University, June 5, 1954

Stevenson was an avid sportsman and fully enjoyed duck hunting trips to California (above) and fishing vacations on small lakes in Wisconsin (below).

If this bountiful land and its richly endowed inhabitants are to meet the challenge of world Communism and world revolution, if they are to withstand the twentieth-century siege of the West, if they are to master the crises of our time, and if they are to press ever forward to great spiritual and material well-being, we desperately need men of vision and competence . . . who are more concerned with tomorrow than yesterday, who, like Thomas Jefferson, prefer "the dreams of the future to the history of the past." . . .

Democratic Rally, Minneapolis, Minnesota, Sept. 25, 1954

The lesson we must now learn is that stabilization is not good enough; moving sidewise is not good enough; a second best year, like a second best poker hand, is not good enough. Even second best in an election isn't good enough, and I'm an authority on that.

Democratic Rally, Detroit, Michigan, Oct. 2, 1954

80

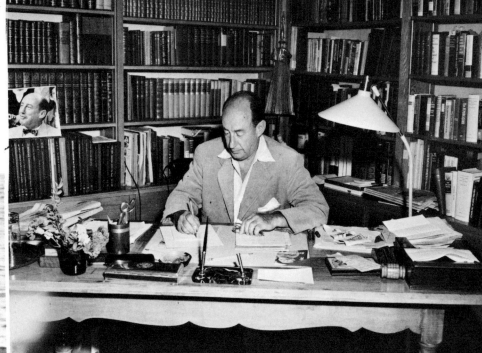

The Stevenson trophy room (above) at Libertyville revealed his family background in political life. Stevenson wrote many of his speeches, articles and books in the study of his farm home (right).

*Stevenson took his son,
John Fell, on a tractor ride during
the summer of 1952.*

*At his christening,
Adlai E. Stevenson IV was held
by his grandfather after the 1956 campaign.*

Ladies and gentlemen, I have just sent the following telegram to President Eisenhower:

"You have won not only the election but also an expression of the great confidence of the American people. I send you my warm congratulations. Tonight we are not Republicans and Democrats, but Americans.

"We appreciate the grave difficulties that your Administration faces, and as Americans we join in wishing you all success in the years that lie ahead." . . .

To you who are disappointed tonight, let me confess that I am, too. But we must not be downhearted, for there is radiance and glory in the darkness could we but see, and to see we have only to look.

For here in America the people have made their choice in a vigorous partisan contest that has affirmed again the vitality of the Democratic process. And I say God bless partisanship, for this is democracy's lifeblood. . . .

. . . The will of our society is announced by the majority. And if other nations have thought in the past few weeks that we were looking the other way, that we were too divided to act, they will learn otherwise.

What unites us is deeper than what divides us.

Love of freedom.

Love of justice.

Love of peace.

May America then continue under God to be the shield and the spear of democracy. And let us give the Administration all responsible support in the troubled times ahead.

Now I bid you good night, with a full heart and a fervent prayer that we will meet often again in the liberal's everlasting battle against ignorance, poverty, misery and war.

I say to you all, everywhere, to be of good cheer, and remember, my dear friends, what a wise man said a long time ago:

"A merry heart doeth good like a medicine, but a broken spirit drieth the bones."

And as for me let there be no tears. If I lost an election, I won a grandchild.

Statement conceding election, Chicago, Illinois, Nov. 10, 1956

. . . The American people have usually blessed the men who dared to look far ahead, to conceive bold plans, to hitch our wagon to a star. But they have soon forgotten men who would weakly settle for the second best.

Democratic Rally, Detroit, Michigan, Oct. 2, 1954

. . . Being in office is like being inebriated. If there are any weaknesses in a man's character it certainly brings them out. . . .

Brooklyn, New York, Oct. 26, 1954

And I beg you, my friends, not to be discouraged. The struggle with evil, error and tyranny is everlasting, but never in vain.

And even the most fanatical ideology must adjust itself to the revealed truths or perish. The job is to cling everlastingly to the truth; to try everlastingly to find it in the chatter and confusion of these times. . . .

Los Angeles, California, Oct. 9, 1954

. . . While I'm in the unique position of one who was born here [California] and left, I can only plead my departure at the age of five was involuntary. I seem to have no more influence on my parents than I had on voters two years ago.

. . . Some may be like the old man down in the Ozarks I heard about the other day.

He was standing to one side, listening attentively to a heated political debate outside the village store. And when one of the combatants said: "Well, Uncle Lave, what's your opinion?" the old man said: "Well, I'll tell you, son: I ain't made up my mind yet how I'm going to vote — but I can tell you this: when I do I sure am going to be bitter."

Los Angeles, California, Oct. 9, 1954

The world at the moment is in a long and dark valley. Science offers us mass suicide. But it also offers the world a greater abundance than we have ever known. Our generation will have to make a fateful choice. . . .

San Francisco, California, Oct. 16, 1954

If ever our system should rise to the highest dignity of its tradition and its responsibilities, it is today. If ever we needed politics which would leave our people informed and united, not confused and divided, it is now. If ever smears, slander, innuendo, misrepresentation were out of place in our national life, it is in this time, at this place, in the world.

Cooper Union, New York, New York, Oct. 30, 1954

Peace is not the work of a single day, nor will it be the consequence of a single act. Yet every constructive act contributes to its growth; every omission impedes it. Peace will come, in the end, imperceptibly, until we realize one day in incredulous surprise that the child is almost grown.

So patience may reward itself. Let us cleanse our minds of the recriminations of the past. Let us abandon the illusion. And as we face — all of us together — a journey into an unknown future, let us recognize that there is no substitute for restraint, honesty and work — yes, and most of all, for the loyalty of Americans to one another. . . .

New Orleans, Louisiana, Dec. 4, 1954

In 1940, Stevenson led the Chicago Committee to Defend America by Aiding the Allies. His wife helped publicize a committee sponsored mass meeting.

Stevenson the politician campaigned in many areas, in many situations (above). His worn shoe (right) became an identification symbol at political rally stops, like the Illinois State Fair (far right).

For it is the primary obligation of democracy's candidates for public office to make democracy work. And I deny the right of any candidate for public responsibility to so debase political discussion that the essential function of the election process is destroyed. There is no right and no reason to poison the wells of people's judgment that their representatives cannot draw from those wells. There is no right to sacrifice on the altar of political ambition that basic harmony between Americans which is essential, once the election is over, to the accomplishment of business of democratic government.

This is serious business. Democracy depends upon giving ideas and principles and policies a chance to fight it out, with time being always on the side of truth. But words, with their appeals to the emotions, striking while the iron is hot, can too often gain the verdict over the best of mind or judgment. The right war cry can win a battle; and a wrong headline can lose a peace. It is not so much that phrases, slogans and epithets dangerously shape public opinion as that they become the cheap substitute for any kind of objective to think when a catch word has already decided for you.

But our problems cannot be solved by epithet, distraction and abuse. . . .

Brooklyn, New York, Oct. 26, 1954

. . . If we exclude the solution of atomic war, and if we exclude the solution of surrender, all we have left is some form of armed truce which we can call co-existence or anything else you like. Armed co-existence is certainly a bleak prospect. But it is better than no existence.

New Orleans, Louisiana, Dec. 4, 1954

Former President Harry S. Truman presented candidate Stevenson to the 1952 Democratic convention in Chicago.

At a 1956 campaign rally, Stevenson was supported by various intellectual groups.

84

I accept your nomination and your program.

I should have preferred to hear those words uttered by a stronger, wiser, better man than myself.

None of you can wholly appreciate what is in my heart. I can only hope that you may understand my words. They will be few.

I have not sought the honor you have done me. I could not seek it because I aspired to another office, which was the full measure of my ambition. One does not treat the highest office within the gift of the people of Illinois as an alternative or a consolation prize.

I would not seek your nomination for the Presidency because the burdens of that office stagger the imagination. It's potential for good or evil now and in the years of our lives smothers exultation and converts vanity to prayer.

I have asked the merciful Father of us all to let this cup pass for me. But from such dread responsibility one does not shrink in fear, in self-interest, or in false humility.

So, "If this cup may not pass away from me, except I drink it, Thy will be done."

That my heart has been troubled, that I have not sought this nomination, that I could not seek it in good conscience, that I would not seek it in honest self-appraisal, it is not to say that I value it the less. Rather it is that I revere the office of President of the United States.

And now that you have made your decision I will fight to win that office with all my heart and soul. With your help, I have no doubt that we will win.

You have summoned me to the highest mission within the gift of any people. I could not be more proud. Better men than I were at hand for this mighty task, and I owe to you and to them every resource of mind and strength that I possess to make your deed of today a good one for our country and our party. I am confident, too, that your selection of a candidate for Vice President will strengthen me and our party immeasurably in the hard, implacable work that lies ahead for all of us.

I know you join with me in gratitude and respect for the great Democrats and leaders of our generation whose names you have considered here in this convention, whose vigor, character and devotion to the Republic have won the respect of countless Americans and enriched our party.

I shall need them, we shall need them, because I have not changed in any respect since yesterday. Your nomination, awesome as I find it, has not enlarged my own capacities. So I shall be profoundly grateful and emboldened by their comradeship and fealty.

Formal Acceptance Speech, Chicago, Illinois, July 26, 1952

85

NGDOM UNITED STATE

Lord Caradon of the United Kingdom and Ambassador Stevenson sat beside each other at the U.N. and had many opportunities to discuss world problems.

. . . It will take a willingness to do together what cannot be done by individuals alone.

It will take, too, a leadership which has faith in the future, and vision, and an understanding of what the people of America really want, and of how much they really want it.

It will take a government which finds its mandates in consideration of the general welfare, and not for any single interest.

It will take a commitment that in our daily lives we live by the Bill of Rights we subscribe to as a nation.

It will take refusal ever to be satisfied, a vision of an America growing ever more beautiful and a freedom ever more complete, a deep conviction in the continued perfectibility of the human spirit.

It will take a full-hearted belief of all of us, that we in America have only just begun to live!

AFL-CIO Convention, New York, New York, Dec. 8, 1955

I can wait until hell freezes over...

. . . The state governments are today playing too passive a role in the urban renewal program. . . .

It seems to me, too, that I have detected reluctance sometimes on the part of officials to work with the private citizens who are seeking to improve their neighborhoods. This is one area in which people are thinking ahead of the times, and every effort should be made to capture the enthusiasm of neighborhood groups for developing conservation programs.

There are real opportunities here for promoting more do-it-yourself-government.

But perhaps our greatest need is to perfect the existing relationship between Government and private enterprise. If the cities are caught in a hurricane of explosive urban growth, it can be said that the public agencies concerned with redevelopment also exist in the eye of another hurricane — a whirlwind of pressure brought to bear by a collection of Washington's most powerful and tireless lobbies. . . .

American Municipal Association Convention, Miami, Florida, Nov. 30, 1955

The new national conservation policy must acknowledge the rule that nature herself provides; the organic unity of the seamless web of land, water, minerals, energy. These are not separate problems to be treated piecemeal, but part of one great problem, one great opportunity that must be treated with comprehensive insight.

November 3, 1956

Stevenson: All right, Sir, let me ask you one simple question: Do you, Ambassador Zorin, deny that the U.S.S.R. has placed and is placing medium- and intermediate-range missiles and sites in Cuba? Yes or no — don't wait for the translation — yes or no?

Valerian Zorin (delegate, U.S.S.R.): I am not in an American courtroom, Sir, and therefore I do not wish to answer a question that is put to me in the fashion in which a prosecutor puts questions. In due course, Sir, you will have your reply.

S.: You are in the courtroom of world opinion right now, and you can answer yes or no. You have denied that they exist — and I want to know whether I have understood you correctly.

Z.: Will you please continue your statement, Sir? You will have your answer in due course.

S.: I am prepared to wait for my answer until hell freezes over, if that is your decision. I am also prepared to present the evidence in this room.

UN Security Council debate on the Cuban missile crisis, New York, New York, Oct. 23, 1962

What should our main objectives in foreign affairs now be? To answer "peace" is to express an aspiration rather than to define a policy. All Americans — all human beings — want nothing more than to live at peace with their brothers. But wishing will not make it so.

To attain peace we must have within ourselves an affirmative vision of hope which we can share with the rest of mankind. We cannot be any stronger in our foreign policy — for all the bombs and guns we may heap up in our arsenals — than we are in the spirit which rules inside the country. Foreign policy, like a river, cannot rise above its source. The image we project to the world will, in the end, reflect what we feel in our minds and hearts.

New Orleans, Louisiana, Dec. 4, 1954

. . . If we employ serious and sensible analysis in place of slick phrases and the techniques of advertising, we will be able better to recognize our problems and make headway with their solution. . . .

New Orleans, Louisiana, Dec. 4, 1954

Let us look first at our strength — our strength in unity, in purpose, in dedication, in productivity; our strength in military equipment, trained manpower and readiness; our strength in the skill and morale of our foreign representatives, in the clarity of our policies and in the nobility of our ideas. Everything which contributes to our strength heartens and encourages our Allies, our friends around the world, and particularly those who would like to be our friends. Everything which contributes to our strength increases the respect and the caution of those who are hostile to us.

New Orleans, Louisiana, Dec. 4, 1954

Let us never forget that self-government was designed for men who had first of all learned to govern themselves.

New Orleans, Louisiana, Dec. 4, 1954

. . . For the weapons man has created can destroy not only his present but his future as well. With the invention of the hydrogen bomb and all of the frightful spawn of fission and of fusion the human race has crossed one of the great warsheds of history, and mankind stands in new territory, in uncharted lands. . . .

Radio Address, Chicago, Illinois, April 11, 1955

. . . The genius of American democracy is that it can produce plain citizens who, when the times demand, can scale the lonely heights of courage and vision.

Dinner honoring Sam Rayburn,
Washington, D. C., April 16, 1955

. . . For healing, like music, is a bridge between races and nations. The secrets of life-giving, unlike those of death-dealing, can be made humanity's possession, binding the giver and the receiver ever closer together.

Bellevue Medical Center, New York, New York,
June 2, 1955

Politicians who can say the right things are a dime a dozen these days. . . . But what pays off is political leadership capable of bold imagination, unafraid to lay its ideas on the line, and unwilling to quit until what has been done is exactly the same size as what has been said. . . .

. . . That words change facts and are a substitute for action reminds me of that poor fellow whose father had died on the gallows. He finally solved his embarrassment by answering whenever anyone asked him about his father: "My late and lamented parent died in consequence of injuries suffered when the floor of the platform gave way during a public ceremony in which he was taking a prominent part."

Democratic Rally, Duluth, Minnesota, Oct. 29, 1955

Group at left and above: In speeches throughout the world, Stevenson stressed human ideals, hopes and goals.

Stevenson's body laid in state in the Illinois capitol building at Springfield.

EPILOGUE

When any man who was as prominent in the affairs of the world as Adlai Stevenson dies suddenly, other prominent people feel called upon to drop some sort of appreciative tribute onto the casket of his memory before it is lowered into the grave.

Understandably, people of varying shades of national and international renown spoke well of Mr. Stevenson in death though they had often, while he was alive, disagreed with his policies and his politics. But, less predictably, a great mass of those who paid their respects spoke with overtones of real sadness in the presence of a real loss.

The things that people felt they had lost with the passing of Adlai Stevenson might have been given different labels by different people, but in sum it was said that he carried the dignity of his own manhood so gracefully that all men were proud of their humanity shared with him.

No one could listen to Mr. Stevenson, or read what he had written, for very long without observing that the Stevensonian ideas grew out of universal ideals, and that they were a part of the man himself and not something wrapped around him for special occasions. What he did, he did because of his convictions. And he arrived at those convictions by travelling the path of justice, not just for his family or his friends, but justice for all. Other men, perhaps equally devoted to the common good, have been, for one reason or another, unheard or misunderstood. But it was Adlai Stevenson's particular excellence that the light of his convictions shone, not only around his own head, but beamed out into the darkness to spotlight obstacles and illuminate the way for the benefit of everyone.

Although Mr. Stevenson would have been amused at the comments of some of those who had opposed him in life and who, in paying tribute to him dead, laced their respectful "in memoriams" with overtones of relief, it is, nevertheless, a gentle mercy that he was spared the humiliation of the defeated tone taken by some of his friends. It would have been small consolation for him to know that some saw in his death the death of some of the things he stood for, and mourned, not only his passing, but the failure of so many of his ambitions.

That he did not do all that he wanted to do is obvious. Who has? But there was a sort of triumph—and most people understood this—in even the attempting of some of the things he tried. It was this triumph that people talked about, using different examples to illustrate it. Some of the people who spoke of him seemed to be trying to fix the memory of the man permanently in their minds and hearts so they might recall it as the need for consolation arose. Some spoke to clarify their observations. Some wrote so that history would remember Stevenson and perhaps remember them for having appreciated him. And almost all of them spoke affectionately.

The words of the great and famous, concerning Adlai Stevenson, have been reported and recorded. They have been printed and are put away in the archives. But a far greater mass of words were spoken by people who weren't thinking of posterity, but were expressing the sudden eloquence of artless emotion.

In the months since his death, the name of Governor Stevenson has come into thousands of conversations. It has entered easily without special pomp or preamble, as a member of the family comes into the living room. On the steps of research libraries, in union hiring halls, in university common rooms, at political dinners and party caucuses, on the bus, on the street, on the beach, in the park, in the store, in the camp, beside the pool, at the dock and in the family-room, there has been a wonderful sameness in the things that seemed to a great variety of people worthy of praise.

The man gestured with his cargo hook. "He came right in here to talk to us as the night gang was coming off. He seemed shorter than I expected, but while he was talking he seemed to get taller."

"He always answered my letters," the old lady said. "I told him when I got to eighty, and he sent me a lovely expensive card. It's in the drawer there. You can see he signed it with his own hand."

The young executive was preoccupied as he crossed behind me and stood looking out across the runway. "If you write about him, don't forget to say that most of us heard him first at a time when the country was fat and stupid and complacent, and knew it, and liked it that way. He got us excited about thinking about who we were, and what we'd done, and what we could do if we'd only get with it.

"He made us proud to be Americans, and glad we were alive right now when so much is going on. Maybe other people had to come along later to get us actually moving, but he started the whole thing. He convinced us that there was someplace to go and some chance of getting there.

"If you write about Stevenson, don't forget to say he woke us up. That's the important thing."

Tributes

I am shocked and saddened at the untimely passing of Adlai Stevenson. His contribution and services to this nation and his distinguished record in the field of foreign relations in our quest for peace will be long remembered by a grateful nation and his friends throughout the world.

Harry S. Truman

The announcement that a public servant of Adlai Stevenson's international stature should be suddenly and finally removed from the world strikes a tragic note for all Americans. As the leader of his party in two Presidential campaigns and as our spokesman at the United Nations in recent years, he has won an abiding place in his country's history. Mrs. Eisenhower and I join all others who love freedom in mourning his untimely passing.

General Dwight D. Eisenhower

I'm just shocked. It's a tremendous loss. He performed the most difficult tasks in the United Nations any American had to perform.

Chief Justice Earl Warren

In the graceful eloquence of his public statements, he had no peers. In two gallant campaigns for the Presidency and as our Ambassador to the United Nations, Adlai Stevenson served his party, his country and the cause of freedom with rare courage, ability and dignity.

Richard M. Nixon

Freedom lost a profoundly great spokesman; more than I can say I am deeply shocked and saddened by his totally unexpected death. Adlai Stevenson was one of the noblest figures to have graced our political life — a public servant of the highest order. We in Illinois benefited immensely from his service as governor and we were proud to have called him our son as he served the nation and the free world. Too, he was my old and cherished friend. I shall miss him greatly — his warmth, his wit, his sincerity, his friendship.

Otto Kerner, Governor of Illinois

His was a life of distinguished public service. He was an articulate spokesman for the cause of human freedom throughout the world.

Nelson A. Rockefeller, Governor of New York

All the world must mourn the loss of a man so dedicated to the cause of peace as Adlai Stevenson. His death comes at a critical time when his remarkable talents and his tireless efforts for the betterment of mankind are sorely needed. I pray that God will reward his selfless service to others and that his soul may find eternal peace.

Francis Cardinal Spellman

Our country should bow in reverence for the passing of a bright star from the horizon of world statesmanship. His leadership was a bright interlude in the troubled history of mankind.

The Rev. Dr. Martin Luther King, Jr.

He embodied in his life rare idealism and practical realities as only few men could have ever done.

Bishop Prince A. Taylor, Jr., President of the
Council of Bishops of the Methodist Church

His passing is an irreparable loss.

Archbishop Iakovos, Greek Orthodox
Primate in the United States

The world has lost one of its most valuable servants.

Rabbi Maurice N. Eisendrath, President,
University of American Hebrew Congregations

As much as any man in our century, Ambassador Stevenson represented a voice of sanity, of compassion, of reason in a tortured world.

He was profoundly aware of the dimensions of man's ancient enemies of hunger, ignorance and disease. He understood the nature of man's inhumanity to man, and he spent his adult life in a courageous struggle to defeat these enemies and to bring light in the application of human intelligence to the conduct of human affairs.

Walter P. Reuther, President of United Auto Workers

His was truly the global point of view, grounded in a profound love of his country and enlightened by compassion for all men.

Dr. Grayson Kirk, President of Columbia University

Mr. Stevenson was a man of quality and he chose to use his gifts of brilliance, of compassion, of persuasion in the service of his nation and the individual human spirit.

Senator Abraham A. Ribicoff

He had a brilliant mind and a great sense of humor. We became very intimate friends. He had some very fine attributes — not merely the cast of his mind, but an idealism that he kept intact. He was a devoted public servant. Adlai Stevenson was one of our great contemporary men.

Senator Everett McKinley Dirksen

All Chicagoans, all of the people of Illinois, and all citizens of the free world are deeply saddened by the untimely death of Ambassador Adlai E. Stevenson. In his passing, I have lost a close colleague and a dear and valued friend.

Illinois and Chicago have given many great men to the nation and to the world, but in our time none greater than Adlai Stevenson.

To most people he was a towering national world figure, but to those among us who knew him best, he was wholly without pretension, always approachable, always interested in not only public, but in the everyday matters affecting the lives of people.

Richard J. Daley, Mayor of Chicago

Adlai Stevenson was a spokesman for humanity. His wisdom, warmth and courage are a legend that will endure and grow with the years to come. He was one of New York City's beloved sons who, despite the great burden of his office, gave unstintingly of his time to scores of good causes. All of us in New York City join his millions of friends throughout the world in mourning his death.

Robert F. Wagner, Mayor of New York City

In the sudden death in London today of Mr. Stevenson the world has lost a great statesman. As an outstanding public figure in his own country, as a candidate for the United States Presidency and as Governor of Illinois he showed a liberality of mind and lucidity of expression which brought him universal renown.

Michael Stewart, Foreign Secretary of Great Britain

Civil rights workers in Chicago gathered in Grant Park to pay tribute to Adlai Stevenson before a summer 1965 march.

It was typical of Mr. Stevenson that he was always ready to listen to what was being said by smaller countries. He was attentive not least to the views of the Nordic countries. The aim of his endeavor was a stable and just peace.

Jens Otto Krag, Premier of Denmark

It is hard to exaggerate the importance of Adlai Stevenson to the free world or to his country. I can only express deep grief and deep shock at the news.

Lester B. Pearson, Prime Minister of Canada

Adlai Stevenson will be mourned by his many friends and admirers in this country.

Sir Alec Douglas-Hume, former Prime Minister
of Great Britain

In the past few days it has been said, over and over again, that Adlai Stevenson was a universal man. And so he was. But not merely because he was informed, well-traveled, urbane, sophisticated, eloquent and gifted; he was all of these. But his universality did not rest upon his being a prince among plain men, but upon his being a plain man even among princes. His was the simplicity of fundamental human values—with what is common in the midst of diversity—with what is permanent in the midst of change: the love of peace; the instinct of tolerance; the feeling of compassion; the devotion to human rights; the urge to act for human welfare.

This philosophy which animated Adlai Stevenson lay deep in him—permanent and indestructible. Perhaps this is what attracted him so powerfully—almost irresistibly—to the United Nations and its noble tasks. For he was committed to the principles of the Charter before it was written. . . .

The words of the Charter—and his own ringing phrases which will live in literature—were more than symbols to him. They were calls to action. He used language as few men have—but used it to summon himself and others to work.

The work to which he summoned our reason and our feelings remains still to be done. The Charter he kept on his desk contains only five pages of philosophy, followed by fifty pages of procedure.

He knew that the philosophy could lift men's vision and sustain their energies. But he also sensed that its meaning was contained not in eloquent words but in agreed procedures, in workable machinery, in arrangements that enabled the nations to work together on particular tasks—while continuing to argue about why they are working together and why they sometimes disagreed.

He had early learned the dictum of Justice Oliver Wendell Holmes that general propositions do not decide concrete cases, and he worked hard and long to build that executive machinery for peace which is the real alternative to the system of war by which men and nations have always lived—by which they no longer dare to live. . . .

There is no institution which deserves such talents more than the United Nations; it calls out for the best that can be produced by the societies of man. Three Presidents of the United States sent Adlai Stevenson to the United Nations. They sent you our best.

Now that he is gone I think of the line from *Pilgrim's Progress:* "So he passed over and all the trumpets sounded for him on the other side." Yet something of him remains with us in this great Assembly hall.

Dean Rusk, Secretary of State (UN Memorial Ceremony)

His understanding of the true causes of present-day problems, his great concern with social affairs, his untiring defence of peace and concord among nations, his knowledge of man and his staunch defence of the ideals in which he believed—all of this manifested in his public acts, in his words, his writing and his actions—had made of him the prototype of the intellectual who uses his culture for the benefit of mankind.

Dr. Carlos Sosa-Rodriguez, Venezuela,
President of 18th Session of UN General Assembly
(UN Memorial Ceremony)

It was himself he gave in word and thought and action, not to his friends alone but to his country, to his world. And the gift had consequences. It changed the tone and temper of political life in the United States for a generation. It humanized the quality of international dialogue throughout a great part of the world. It enlightened a dark time.

Which means, I suppose, that Adlai Stevenson's great achievement was himself. What we have lost as he said of his friend Mrs. Roosevelt, is not his life. He lived that out, if not to the full, at least more fully than almost any other man. What we have lost is himself. And who can name the warmth and richness of it?

Archibald MacLeish (UN Memorial Ceremony)

This ceremony has ended.
The memory and influence of Adlai
Stevenson have not ended.
Francis T. P. Plimpton, U. S. Delegation
(UN Memorial Ceremony)

Statement by
U.N. Secretary General U Thant
at the Stevenson
Memorial Ceremony

When I first was told last Wednesday, a little before 1:00 p.m., that Ambassador Stevenson had died in London, I could not believe my ears. I had seen him only recently, in Geneva, less than a week before and he was so alive, and looked so well. When the news was confirmed, it took me some time to accept the fact that Adlai Stevenson had really passed away.

My first thought was to send a message of condolences to President Johnson. In my message I referred to the respect, admiration and affection of all of his colleagues at the United Nations which Ambassador Stevenson had earned over the last four and a half years by reason of his extraordinary human qualities.

The same afternoon I referred, in a public statement, to my sense of grief and shock because, suddenly and without warning, death had struck and we had lost a good friend and a highly esteemed colleague. As I stated in that tribute, in his years at the United Nations, Ambassador Stevenson had demonstrated with rare distinction how it was possible to combine the highest form of patriotism with loyalty to the idea of international peace and co-operation.

When on 8 December 1960, it was announced that Mr. Stevenson was to be Permanent Representative of the United States of America to the United Nations, it seemed to everybody to be such a natural and right appointment. He was, in truth, one of the founding fathers of the United Nations, having been present at the signing of the Charter in San Francisco in June 1945, and also having been closely associated with the negotiations leading up to that historic event.

Thereafter, he was the head of the United States Delegation to the Preparatory Commission and Executive Committee of the United Nations in London, and I believe his offices were located in Grosvenor Square, close to the very spot where he collapsed last Wednesday. . . .

I remember how many tributes were paid to him when he took over his duties at the United Nations. There were so many encomiums, both within and outside these walls, that they could have turned the head of a lesser man. Not so with Ambassador Stevenson. On one occasion he observed: "Flattery is like smoking — it is not dangerous so long as you do not inhale."

During the four and a half years that he served at the United Nations, he stood as the embodiment of dedication to the principles of the United Nations. His many speeches, which expressed so well his whole mental and intellectual approach, in the championship of fundamental rights, in defence of the dignity and worth of the human person, in support of the equal rights of nations large and small, were cheered and applauded by all sides of the house. He not only spoke with a rare gift of phrase, but with such an obvious sincerity that his words carried conviction....

There were some during his lifetime, of course, who rated him as too liberal and too far ahead of the times. Others sought to discount his effectiveness on the score that he was too much the idealist and therefore not practical enough. This does him injustice.

The line of distinction between idealism and vision is obscure at best. Vision, certainly, is an essential attribute of statesmanship, and he was a fine statesman. In any case, what a dismal world it would be, and how unpromising its future, without spiritual lift given to mankind by the idealists who, in the courage of their conviction, chart the course and mark the goals of man's progress! ...

From the time that Mr. Stevenson became the Permanent Representative of his country at the United Nations and while I was still the Permanent Representative of Burma, we developed very close ties of friendship. These ties became even closer towards the end of the year when I assumed my present responsibilities, and continued to be so during the last three and a half years. I found it easy to discuss with him any current issue of importance with complete freedom, and in full frankness and friendliness.

No one can serve his country in the United Nations for long without having his moments of frustration. Ambassador Stevenson had his share of such moments, and on such occasions he confided to me his innermost thoughts, and I was struck by his completely human approach to our common problems. He seemed not only to think about them, but also to feel about them as a human being. In all such discussions I was repeatedly impressed by his dedication to the basic concepts of peace, justice and freedom.

So many tributes have been paid to Mr. Stevenson since his sudden and tragic passing away. So many of his friends and admirers have eulogized his fine intellect, his modesty and humility. Many have praised his felicitous style and his ready wit. Tributes have been paid to his great learning, which he carried so lightly because he was truly an educated man, a

cultured man, a civilized man. . . .

Unfortunately, Adlai Stevenson is no longer with us to keep step with us in the march forward to the goals he had stated so well.

On this occasion when we are paying homage to the memory of one who has left us so large a legacy, it is fitting, I believe, to give some thought to the momentous questions of war and peace which were so close to his heart.

In my view, many governments, while unwilling to wage war, and at the same time unable to make peace, seem to have resigned themselves to the prospect of an interminable cold war. While admittedly the cold war cannot bring down the physical holocaust on our heads, it has nevertheless already inflicted on us a tremendous moral and psychological injury which is intangible but equally destructive. The long, uneasy cold war has destroyed and mutilated not our bodies, but our minds. Its weapons are the myths and the legends of propaganda.

It has often been said that in war, the first casualty is truth. The cold war is also capable of inflicting the same casualty. The weapons designed and utilized to crush and mutilate the human mind are as potent as any of the weapons designed for physical destruction. The weapons of the cold war contaminate our moral fibre, warp our thinking processes and afflict us with pathological obsessions. These are the invisible but, nevertheless, the most devastating effects of the cold war on humanity. I believe Adlai Stevenson, in his innermost thoughts, realized these truths.

There is no doubt that Adlai Stevenson has earned a place in history — not only a place in the history of his own country, but a place in the history of this world Organization. He brought to international diplomacy, in his dignity, his gentility and his style, a special dimension. Even more, he has earned the admiration and affection of millions of people to whom he was but a name and a legend.

This was so, I think, because so often his voice rang true as the voice of the people, his eloquence expressed the hopes and aspirations of the common man the world over. He was, in our times, in a quite unique way, the people's friend. Equally, he has earned a permanent place in the hearts of all those who knew him, and today I mourn his passing, not just as a great historical figure, a famous man, but as a true and trusted friend. As the poet says: "Friendship is a nobler thing; Of friendship it is good to sing."

AFTERWORD

The Double Legacy of Adlai Stevenson

We will all miss Adlai Stevenson. We will miss him at the United Nations. We will miss his wit and wisdom on those many occasions when Americans gather together in convention to view the world and their relation to it.

We will miss his splendid words, written and spoken, and — more than that — we will miss his personal dedication to the high principles of democracy about which he wrote and spoke.

We will miss him as a friend: for every American, whether he agreed or disagreed with Governor Stevenson's programs, admired the Governor as a human being and a fellow citizen, and admired his principles, and wished him well.

Yet great as is our sadness at the loss of this great American, it is important for us to recall how frighteningly much all Americans, and all freemen everywhere, would have lost if Adlai Stevenson had chosen to remain aloof from the problems of his country and his age, and, instead of becoming directly and vitally involved, had chosen to withdraw simply into the backwash of criticism.

Governor Stevenson was not simply a thinker or a master of words; he was also a do-er and a maker. He did not simply see a vision and then lapse into contemplation or discussion, but he arose and walked towards the ideal, and worked for it, and urged his fellow Americans to stand and walk with him.

He was, in short, and in the fullest and happiest sense, a man of politics. And, by his intellect and his integrity, he elevated the definition of the word "politician" and raised the world's opinion concerning men of political action.

He has left us. And we will miss him. But he has left us a double legacy: he has left us his words to reflect upon, and he has left us his memory to be our inspiration.

HUBERT H. HUMPHREY
Vice President